The Thinking Golfer's Manual

WHAT AMATEURS NEED TO KNOW

Steve Koch

ThinkingManBooks
Montgomery, Texas

Cover Design by Cathi Stevenson, www.BookCoverExpress.com

Book Layout © 2017 BookDesignTemplates.com

Photography by David W. Clements / dwc photography
Photo Editing by E. J. Taul

Golf Channel is a trademark of TGC, LLC.
Golf Digest is a trademark of Advance Magazine Publishers, Inc.
Golf Magazine is a trademark of TI Golf Holdings Inc.
Golf Pride is a trademark of the Eaton Corporation.
LPGA is a service mark of the Ladies Professional Golf Association.
PGA, PGA Tour and *These Guys are Good* are trademarks of The
Professional Golfers' Association of America.
Shell's Wonderful World of Golf is a trademark of the Shell Oil Company.
The notched, white and black two-tone, clubhead design is a trademark of the
Taylor Made Golf Company.
USGA is a service mark of the United States Golf Association.

ThinkingManBooks
20821-D Eva Street, No. 57
Montgomery, Texas 77356-1889
ThinkGreatGolf@SPKoch.com

An earlier version of this book was privately published in a limited edition
titled *Uncle Steve's Guide to Golf*, © 2016 Stephen Koch.

Library of Congress Control Number: 2018901396

The Thinking Golfer's Manual/Stephen Koch, 1st Ed.
ISBN 978-0-9995621-0-9

I give much credit for my love of this game to a small paperback gift from my parents many years ago: The Arnold Palmer Method. *They, and he, got me into this, for which I am eternally thankful.*

Table of Contents

Table of Mulligans

Table of Photographs

Preface

Let's start with three basic questions: Why another golf book? Why *The Thinking Golfer's Manual?* Why should you listen to what I have to say?

First question first: Why another golf book? In fact, why are there so many golf books already available? It is simple really—golf is the only game one person does alone, without a partner. Golfers practice every aspect of the game alone; unlike any other sport. Golfers play alone—against another player, yes, but primarily alone against the golf course; again, unlike any other sport. The mental challenges golf poses are unlike those posed by any other sport. Period.

Combine those realities with the fact every golfer is unique in his or her own way, and the number of golf books on the market is not a surprise. Each is merely a logical attempt to address golf and golfer uniqueness. This book is no different. The pages that follow cover subjects you may have read about elsewhere, perhaps even in much the same words. Those pages also cover subjects in rather different words than you have read elsewhere. In all cases, the words you will read result from my more than fifty years of playing and studying the game; I hope their substance will help you improve your game.

Second: Why *The Thinking Golfer's Manual?* Golf involves the practice of a single player against his or her own mental and physical strengths and weaknesses. There is no other player on the field to pick up the slack when a golfer makes a mistake. For that reason golf requires more intellectual and emotional brain control than any other sport. Golf requires clear unemotional thinking about each shot—what type of shot it is, what is required to carry it off, and what strategy is required in the context of the hole being played. That level of thinking is particularly important on the practice range, where golfers must train their mind and body to repeat swings without conscious thought. The practice range is where the habits that make a good golf game are developed. Golfers must know when to think about the shot to be played next, and when to rely on the habits developed during their hours of practice to carry out the shot.

Finally: Why should you listen to what I have to say? Fair question. In addition to the emotional brain control golf requires, it also requires the intellectual capacity to analyze the game, to analyze the shots to be carried out, and to analyze the swings required for those shots. As a trained research scientist, first, and an experienced intellectual property and international lawyer, second, I have spent a lifetime analyzing a wide variety of challenges and problems. As a relaxing sidelight over those many years, I have also analyzed the golf swing. This book is a result of those years of analysis.

There is more though. Just as each golfer is unique, each golf writer is unique. I have tried to write in a voice I have not seen in other golf books, and sometimes in words other golf books have not used. Those differences are intentional, as my amateur perspective is different from the perspective of authors with a professional golf background. I am trying to communicate at the level of the amateurs that will be reading this book.

Here is an example of how I have tried to address a complicated subject which is frequently difficult for amateur golfers to understand. Ben Hogan's classic short text *Five Lessons—The Modern Fundamentals of Golf*, first published in *Sports Illustrated* in the 1950s, and Tom Watson's much underappreciated book *Getting Back to Basics*, both spend pages on the hand and wrist positions in the backswing. Those pages are difficult to fully understand, at least they were for me. In developing the chapter addressing that subject, I came up with a new approach to understand the hand and wrist positions we should all strive for. I hope this new approach aids your understanding of this important subject. You will find other new ways to think about your golf swing in these pages, all of which together make up, and are why I have written, *The Thinking Golfer's Manual*.

Photos accompany the text where a new approach to understanding what the golf swing requires is described. Photos are also included where the old adage "A picture is worth a thousand words" is clearly applicable. You may be surprised, however, to find that not every chapter of this book has photos. There is logic on this point as well.

As suggested by the book's title, great golf requires, yes, thinking. The requirement to think starts with every part of what it takes to successfully complete a golf shot—picturing the shot to be played, getting the stance and grip correct, starting and finishing the swing, and all the rest of what the game has to it. In some areas, reading this book without pictures will force detailed thought about the message the words are trying to convey. That detailed thinking will help you develop the good technical habits that are needed to develop a reliable golf game. The task of thinking is also what is required on the golf course. It is best to start now.

A second reason is that today's onslaught of digital media leads to a life where we are all overwhelmed with information. We can easily find high quality pictures of professionals in virtually every position we might require for study of the game. After studying any part of the text, whether a picture is included or not, find appropriate pictures or videos of professional golfers on the internet pages of your choice. You will find that there is much available from which we can all learn.

The professional golfers I use for examples are generally older golfers, on the Champions tour or perhaps even retired. Writing a book is a long, arduous process and those golfers were not, and nor was the author, quite so old when the project of writing *The Thinking Golfer's Manual* began.

In addition, the golfing public is familiar with the top players on the tours today; that familiarity may make it harder to think about what is in this book without being biased by what you have seen or heard on television or from other media. The purpose of this book, one of them anyway, is to get you to think about your game, not think about Jason Day's, or Jordan Spieth's, or Dustin Johnson's game. A lack of familiarity with the subjects of my examples should force more thought about the examples and how they apply to your game. Which is what I want to happen.

You will find I have included *Mulligans* between the chapters of this book. These *Mulligans* are short bits of information about the golf game not fitting into any single chapter, but include thoughts I wanted to convey.

A brief note on my sources. I have long been a *Golf Digest* and *Golf Magazine* reader, and over the years have developed the habit of cutting out and saving clippings of key instructional material for later reference. This book is therefore a combination of my own observations, some of the better advice from those clippings (by which I mean the advice tending to be constant over the years, and not varying with the whims of the golfing public's enthusiasm with the subtle, sometimes unusual, aspects of a now-or-then hot tour golfer's swing), and here and there what I have learned from the various books on my bookshelf. It goes without saying this book benefits more than I can say from the professionals I have taken lessons from over the years.

No doubt some of what follows has been suggested, consciously or not, by internet-derived material, including emails from various online golf magazines and *The Golf Channel*. There is more on how all these sources led to this book being what it is in the last chapter.

As all authors say, however, any errors or failures are unintentional and solely mine.

Stephen Koch

October, 2017

How to Use This Book

As you have just read, golf is a complicated game, golfers are unique, and, if to be mastered, golf requires thinking. A fair question for you to ask is "How should I go about using this book to improve my game?"

My scientific and legal research background trained me to take on all tasks in a logical manner; an approach I recommend to you. First, read this book cover to cover, not necessarily all in one sitting because the subject matter is complicated in some areas. As you read, take notes about your own swing—both when you think you are doing something correctly, and when you realize there is something you should work on.

When you have finished reading, review those notes and decide what you want to focus on, and in what order. You may to alternate practice sessions, e.g. start with a full swing issue, then go to a putting or chipping green to practice something related to that part of the game. Changing around sessions in that manner keeps practice from getting too regimented and, in the worst case, boring.

In fairness to all golfers—I am right-handed – I wrote this book in a manner which hopefully will be equally useful to both right and left-handed golfers. When I use the word forward, in reference, for example, to a foot, leg, arm, or other body part, I am referring to the side of the body facing the target, e.g. a right-handed golfer's left side. For a left-handed golfer, I obviously mean the right side. The words back and backward refer to the side of the body away from the target—the right side for a right-handed golfer, and the left side for a left-handed golfer. I occasionally use descriptions corresponding only to a right-handed golfer, in particular in the *Grip* chapter, but only when I thought the subject matter would be most clearly understood by doing so.

I use the words front and rear to refer to the side of the golfer facing the target line, or to the rear of the golfer, respectively. Finally, with respect to hand position on the club, I use upper and lower in reference to hand position on the club, meaning, for example, respectively, the right and left hands for a left-handed golfer.

You will note that I refer to my friends—anonymously except in one case where I had permission to use a name—in a number of stories of golfers doing things they should, or should not, do. No doubt some of you will wonder if you are the subject matter of the stories. I can only say that in most, but to be honest not all, of these stories I have adjusted the facts so as not to directly praise, or offend, anyone in particular. If you think you are my subject matter, well, maybe that is a good thing. You decide.

However you choose to use this book, I hope you enjoy what I have written and find it useful for improving your game. I also hope that it helps you enjoy many more years of playing this great sport.

Philosophizing

I have played golf for a long time. The people I play with generally think I hit the ball a long way and I do compared to many of them. For most of my life, though, I've not been a long hitter, and was frequently the shortest hitter in my group. At times that was irritating, but, as the phrase goes "They don't put your driving distance on the scorecard."

The advantage I always had, and usually still have, is I know almost exactly how long each of my clubs will go if hit as intended. I have lost a few yards as I have aged, and technology has changed all of our distances, but until recently I could count on my seven iron being 153 yards, plus or minus two or three yards depending on temperature, humidity, and the like. Higher numbered clubs were sequentially ten yards less, lower numbered clubs were sequentially ten yards more. So I knew my nine iron was the club for a 130-135 yard approach to the green, and my four iron was the club for a shot in the low 180s.

A golfer has to know his game. That knowledge starts with knowing how long he hits each club.

For quite a few years before I retired one of our senior managers sponsored an afternoon golf outing. Four or five afternoons a year those of us whose business and work schedules allowed got away from the office for a round. It was casual golf, a bit of competition of course, but mostly comradery and team building. It was a great way to get to know colleagues in other office locations.

One year I was paired with a younger attorney from the same office I was working in at the time. He had not played much golf, but was young and flexible and his swing was not terrible. His lack of play, however, gave him an unreliable swing.

We came to a par three, about 165 yards long. A good hole having a kidney-shaped green; the pin was on the front right, accessible but challenging. The bank of the green dropped off to the right rather quickly and there was water short and left, though not in play.

A six iron off the tee was the correct club for me, and I hit a good shot. My colleague then asked "Steve, what club did you use?"

I told him "I used my 165 yard club."

He repeated himself "But Steve, what club did you use?"

I tried to explain he should use the club he thought he could reliably hit 165 yards. He should not be guided by what club I had used.

My explanation was for naught; I told him I used a six iron. He got out his six iron and promptly hit his tee shot short of the green by ten or twenty yards, dangerously close to the water.

A golfer has to know his game. That knowledge means using the club that is right for him, not for one of the other players in his group.

There is a corollary to the "Pick the club that is right for you" rule. The corollary addresses shots where distance should not be the only consideration.

Consider the chipping and pitching part of the golf game. I play with several golfers who follow a two-step process for picking the club they will use when they are near the green: (1) How long do I have from my ball to the pin? (2) It's less than X yards so the club to use must be the sand wedge. The value of "X" changes from golfer to golfer, but you get the idea.

Here is a better golfer's analysis: (1) How long do I have from my ball to the pin? (2) How much of that distance is green, and how much of it is first cut, second cut, fairway, or rough? (3) How short is the grass that is not the green, and how wet or dry is it? (4) How much of an elevation change do I have between where my ball is and where the pin is? (5) How quick are the greens today? (6) Does the green slope toward my ball or away from it? Etc. etc. etc. You, again, get the idea.

Raymond Floyd, a Hall of Fame golfer who played from the 1970s to the 1990s, was known to use any club from a four iron up to his sand wedge for approach shots to the pin. His success speaks for itself—four majors and more than 60 other wins worldwide. More recently, Tiger and Phil have occasionally played short shots from the first or second cut with a hybrid.

The message here is to look at the shot to be played, and find the way to play it that maximizes the likelihood the result will be a success. A wedge is not always the club to use.

The short game is best played if all clubs in your bag are considered to be potential weapons in your armory.

I heard a story a number of years ago, perhaps true, perhaps apocryphal, but in either case making a good point all golfers should think about. As the story goes, Davis Love III was one of the longest hitters on tour when he first earned his playing card, but was not immediately successful—he hit the ball long, but not reliably straight. He figured out, or someone told him, he needed to make a choice—was he going to be a long hitter or a straight hitter? He retooled his swing a bit, and came back as a long, but not quite as long, and much straighter hitter, and his career took off.

A few years later John Daly hit the tour with his first big win, the PGA Championship at Crooked Stick, a course outside of Indianapolis. He of course has always had a big swing and body turn, the result being an ability to hit all of his clubs phenomenal distances. He had success as well, winning The Open Championship in addition to the PGA.

But Daly—let's forget his personal issues for a moment (I recently read a book he wrote a number of years ago; there is another side to the stories we have always heard)—did not have the success he probably would have liked. One reason could be he never sorted out whether he wanted to be a long hitter, or a not quite as long but straighter hitter (I may be stepping out on a limb making that statement, but it works to make my point—keep reading).

You may know, or will meet, golfers with this challenge. I have a good friend who has always been a much longer hitter with all his clubs than I have ever been. He also has always had at least twice the handicap I have.

Golfers have to make decisions about what kind of game they want to have—a game adapted to maximize the likelihood of regularly having good scores, as Davis Love did, or a powerful game that is impressive but not necessarily conducive to reliably good scoring—like John Daly.[1]

Thinking about the distance the ball will go with each club reminds me of a round I played at a golf resort in central Florida not long ago. I was playing

---

[1] In addition to stepping out on a limb with what I have said about John Daly, I have not been able to find a recent source confirming the accuracy of Davis Love's golf history, which I first heard while watching a televised professional tournament a number of years ago. If it is inaccurate, my apologies to Davis Love III.

a vacation round with a good friend and he was having trouble getting the distances with his clubs he expected to get. I remember one specific exclamation, after he hit a tee shot with his driver, "What is going on? I always hit this club at least 280 yards!"

You probably know what I am going to say next. Let's be honest, most of us never hit our driver that distance more than once a month or so, and only then if we are lucky. So, let's get serious, shall we?

My friend lives in a different part of the country, and I do not know what condition his home course is in. The fairways may be dry and hard, providing yards of roll on well-hit drives. With that roll he might hit the ball 280 yards more often than would otherwise be expected. The course condition in Florida was certainly not dry and hard, though, and on this day 280 yards off the tee was what we should only have been dreaming about.

There are two points to be made. First, be honest with yourself about your distances—get a range finder and work the problem hard the next time you are on the range. Club selection becomes easy when we know the distance each club gives us.

Second, there will be days when a club, say your seven iron, which typically sends the ball out say 155 plus or minus 3 yards, comes up 8 or 10 yards short. And you stand there and wonder "I thought I hit the ball well, why is it short?" It may be you did not hit the ball as well as you thought, or perhaps the distance estimate was wrong, or perhaps something else was going on and it turns out to be a one-time event that day. But if it occurs again and again, what to do?

What to do, to analogize using a phrase from Wall Street, is "Don't fight the tape." The next time you have the same distance take the next longer club and get the ball on the green. Scores are not based on the club used, so don't let your ego get in the way. Figure out on the range what is going on with your distances. Not an issue to solve on the course.

This issue arises more frequently with age. If you have never had this problem, be prepared.

If you have read the book *The Tipping Point* (which you should do), you will know one of the points the author makes is there is a single consistent characteristic in the background of people who are the most successful in their chosen profession. Specifically, they have typically spent at least 10,000 hours developing the skills they needed for their profession. Bill Gates is one example. He was fortunate to have access to early generation computers in the schools he attended; by the time he started at Harvard he had spent at least that many hours programming computers. The book has other examples, each leading to the same conclusion: To get to the top, practice is required.

Let's think about the average professional golfer. Let's say he gets serious about golf at age ten, which is later than most do get serious. Let's also say that 250 days a year he practices three hours a day, during which he hits 200 balls. By the time he is 18 1/2, about the average age for a college freshman on the first day of class, he has hit 250 times 200 times 8 ½ balls in 3 times 250 times 8 1/2 hours.

That's a lot more than 10,000 balls hit in a lot less than 10,000 hours. Add all the balls they hit during their college years, and all the rounds they play in the years leading up to college graduation, is it any wonder *These Guys are Good?*

We are never going to be able to get to ten thousand hours of practice, given everything else we have to do in life. But if the pros practice that much to get that good, shouldn't we practice more than we usually do to get better than we presently are?

A friend of mine has paid much more on lessons over the course of our lifetimes than I have even dreamed of paying. He has also played many more rounds than I have. But guess what? He does not go to the range and practice as much as I do. Guess what else? Who do you think has the lower handicap, and almost invariably has the lower score when we play together?

Golf is a game of repetition. Golf is a game requiring practice. Go to the range; the results will be apparent on your scorecards.

A golf mentor of mine, long ago when I was young and better able to play the game than I am now, once told me "To score well you need to avoid double bogeys." He didn't say it but he also meant to stay away from penalty strokes, because they almost invariably lead to double bogeys or worse. He could not have been more right.

In most rounds amateurs play, a "do or die" shot arises for their score on at least one hole. Those shots bring another important aspect of the mental part of the game into play. Do we need to make the attempt, and risk our score for the hole, or should we take the safe option, minimize the chance we will end up with a double bogey or worse, and thus perhaps preserve our chance of having a good overall score for the round?

When those shots arise think about what kind of round you are playing. Are you out alone, working on your game, or is it a regular game with friends in which the end result is more important than the success in pulling off the miracle shot? If the former, give it a go and see what you learn. If the latter, take the safe route.

These are easy words to write; but hard thoughts to implement. In the heat of a round we all forget the simple mental rules we should be following. In my experience, the miracle shot versus safe route decision is the first one we forget. Another example of why the mental part of golf is so important.

The *USGA Golf Handicap System* allows everyone to compete on an equal footing. The handicap rules are not in the *Rules of Golf*, but rather can be found on the *USGA* website. We are to turn in our scorecard if we play thirteen or more holes; the website tell how to estimate scores for the holes that were not played.

Anyone who has played golf very long will know of golfers who always seem to play better than their handicaps. As a result they are usually near the top of the casual tournaments many of us enjoy playing in. Golf is a game of ethics and honesty, including a fairly reported handicap. Turn your scorecards in—don't be one of those golfers others wonder about.

My brother-in-law, who has given me permission to print this quote, tells of a day long ago when I turned to him and said "Jeff, there are two or three proper ways for a golfer to grip the club, and you don't do any of them!"

I don't remember that day or statement, but I probably said it.

This book covers the entire swing and certain specific types of shots; you will have to figure out what to incorporate into your game now, what to incorporate later, and what you may never incorporate. You will read that message over and over again. But what should you do on a typical day on the course?

Let's say you are out with your usual gang for a round and nothing is going as it usually does. You cannot figure out what is wrong, but your game seems to be out of sorts. What should you think about to try and correct that day's problems?

If, for example, you use Jeff's "unapproved method of gripping the club," check to see if you are gripping the club as usual and if so move on—something else must be the problem that day. Do not try to adjust to one of the approved grip styles; wait until a practice range session. If you are doing something like you always do it, but your score is higher than usual, the problem that day is something else.

So what kind of things might we need to look at during a round to try to get the scorecard to look better on the remaining holes? The answer to that question will be different for each of us, but I have written this book in a way I hope will enable you to find your own answer.

For example, I have always had a problem maintaining proper alignment of my stance with the target line. I also have to work on maintaining my rhythm and tempo. Those are the kind of things I can check in real-time to make adjustments to my game during a round. Perhaps your issue will be ball position in the stance. Perhaps it will be how your body is positioned at address. I have written about all of these topics, and more, in the pages of this book.

When bad days on the course come, as they do for all of us, only make changes to things you are doing different than usual. All the rest, the fundamental changes that need to be made, should be reserved for the range.

Until a few decades ago the message given to golfers was that weight training was to be avoided but flexibility exercises were essential. When Tiger Woods hit the tour the message changed, and today's golfers—Jason Day is an obvious example—are incredibility fit physically. What should the average golfer do to maintain his golf fitness? What exercises should be part of a golfer's practice routine?

Golf doesn't require a rigorous day-to-day exercise program, but the game is more enjoyable for those who are in good shape. You know that. Strength in the muscles key to the golf swing are what give golfers distance and consistency. You know that too. A good workout regimen should have three objectives:

Flexibility

The golf swing requires flexibility—particularly in the muscles and joints of the back, shoulders, and hips. Exercises in this category will be familiar to anyone in good physical condition; familiarity, however, should not make you think less of their importance. (I recall seeing a picture of Greg Norman, in his pre-round warm-up, nearly touching his chin against his shins from a standing position. If flexibility will get me closer to having his swing, sign me up.) Examples to consider are back and hamstring stretches, trunk rotations, and hip flexor stretches.

Strength

A weightlifters physique is not necessary to be a good golfer, but good muscle tone and strength is important. Distance and consistency require strong muscles in the back, shoulders, abdomen, and legs. Not to mention the forearms and wrists. The usual exercises we all hate to do are all that is needed here—sit-ups, push-ups, leg raises, lunges, and knee bends.

Muscle Coordination/Control

The golf swing involves a unique combination of activities requiring muscle coordination and control; a good exercise program should include activities which develop the necessary swing-specific strengths and habits. If you have access to a fitness facility, weight-counter-balanced cable motion machines are good for golf fitness.

All golfers should add a fourth category—the pre-round warm-up routine. Although it involves activities which are included in the above three—in particular the flexibility examples—this routine is important to the start of the round, and in particular for minimizing the likelihood of injury during the round. Every golfer should come up with a warm-up routine to regularly follow to get ready for his rounds.

The bottom line, though, is that exercise is not the purpose of this book and great physical fitness is not essential to enjoy the game. Yes, today's great golfers are in great physical shape. But look back over the years at Hall of Fame golfers—Jack Nicklaus when he started his professional career and Billy Casper later in the 1960s—and more recent tour players—Craig "The Walrus" Stadler in the 1990s, and his nearly mirror image son, and the cigar-smoking European golfer Miguel Angel Jimenez. None exemplified, or exemplify, great physical specimens.

What they all had in common though were great golf minds—the ability to think through the game, to find a swing thought that worked for them, to make the situational decisions that applied to each shot they had to carry out. My goal in *The Thinking Golfer's Manual* is to provide the information you need to develop that same ability.

Enough philosophizing. Let's get to the good stuff.

Mulligan

Agree With Me, or Not

"Writer's Prerogative" and "Editorial Discretion" are well-known phrases in the publishing industry. The essential message of each is that he who sits behind the keyboard has the right and power to press the keys he wants to press.

So it is with this book. Golf in many ways is a rather straightforward game; in other ways a very complicated game. The fact there are so many golf books, magazines and commentators tells me that for most amateur golfers it is more often the latter than the former.

You will not agree with everything I have written. That's OK. But as with any work intended to be both educational and entertaining whether one agrees is not the point. In golf as in life one can learn much by reading words with which one may disagree.

If you find what I have written is helpful—great. If not, but something else is, that is also great.

The bottom line message: Work is required to develop the habits necessary to develop a reliable golf game. Whether you read it here or not, do not give up too soon; mastery of even the smallest part of this game takes time.

The Basics

The Grip

Have you noticed how slow motion replays during televised golf tournaments are accompanied by detailed analyses of virtually every aspect of the golf swing, but rarely focus on the grip?

Professional golfers all use the same basic grip. If all amateurs used the same grip, I would not have to write this chapter. But in fact, the single biggest weakness in the average amateur's game is the grip. No other part of the game has more potential to improve golf scoring consistency.

Placing the Hands on the Club Correctly

Golf books and magazine articles talk about images of parallel hands, V's pointing to the right shoulder, and the like. I'll give you a new image—the three knuckles visible grip. Here are my four steps to a good golf grip (this is one of the subjects I have written about from the perspective of a right-handed golfer):

1) Hold your left hand with the fingers points up, palm facing away from you. With a pen or marker, make small circular spots just below the first knuckle of each of the first three fingers. Do the same for the first two knuckles of the right hand. The size of the spots you should use will partially depend on how large your hands are, as will be apparent in the next several paragraphs.

2) Point your left arm downward, palm up. Lay the club on top of the base of the second, third, and fourth fingers (in other words, so each finger is entirely visible). The club should extend across the lower part of the first finger; the base of the finger should be visible. Now

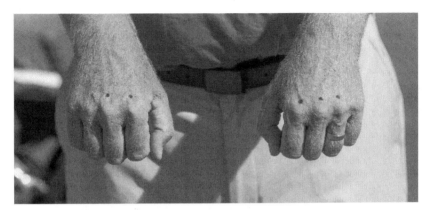

Marking the hands for the three knuckles visible grip technique.

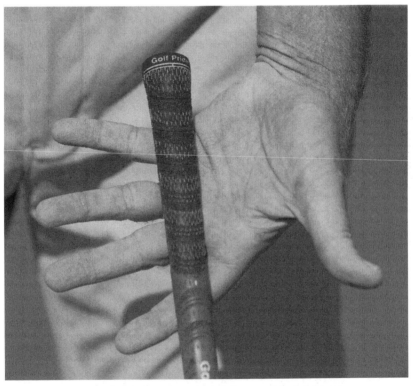

Placing the club on the palm and fingers of the left hand.

fold the fingers over the club to complete the left hand grip. The left thumb should point toward the clubhead but be slightly to the right of the top of the shaft. A good test to determine if the left thumb is in the correct place is whether the meat at the base of the palm side of the thumb (which is called the thumb pad) is just a bit to the right of the top of the shaft. Take care not to unnaturally extend the thumb to the right or press it close to the first finger. Grip the club by applying pressure with the last three fingers only. The first finger and thumb should feel as if they are merely along for the ride.

Stand as if you were addressing a ball with the club on the ground. You should clearly see the first two black spots, but just a bare hint of the third spot.

Make sure the club sits naturally on the ground, so the lie angle of the clubhead determines the angle the shaft makes with the ground. This is important—many golfers do not allow the clubhead to sit naturally on the ground after the club has been gripped, or turn the clubhead while addressing the ball. Your ball contact will not be consistent if the clubhead does not sit on the ground at its lie angle or is not square to the ball at address.

3)   The right hand may be harder to correctly put into position. Place the little finger of the right hand between the first and second fingers of the left hand. It should rest against the side of the first finger and barely touch the second finger.

4)   Fold the right hand over the left, so the right thumb pad extends over the left thumb and is partly between the thumb and first finger of the left hand. The right thumb will be to the left of the top of the shaft, with only the second and third fingers applying pressure to the club. Stand once more as if you were addressing a ball. You should see the first, but only a bit of the second, black mark on the right hand.

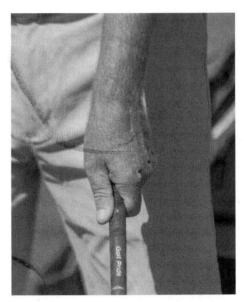

The left hand grip.

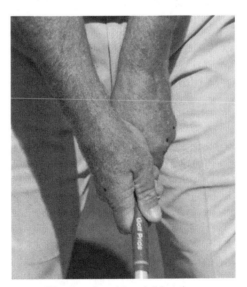

The three knuckles visible grip.

Note on the Proper Grip

Most golf writers say the club should lie in the fingers, and not the palm, of the upper hand. I don't necessarily disagree, but I think the method I described above is better for the average golfer. The three knuckles visible technique is an easier way to consistently grip the club correctly, as opposed to thinking about whether the club is in the fingers or the palm of the hand. It also makes it easier to maintain a proper upper hand position when gripping the club with the lower hand. After time, the club will feel properly balanced between the fingers and the palm of the upper hand.

At first, though, this grip will seem unnatural—primarily in the lower hand, which you will want to turn to the back (particularly if you have played using another grip, for example a baseball or softball-style grip, for a long time). But an unnatural feeling means it is correct; it is the grip you want to have. It is the grip on which all good golfers rely—your game will be well served if you focus on the three knuckles visible technique until it becomes second nature.

When I first tried this grip, it felt unnatural and was hard to get used to. I learned it from my instructor, mentor, and neighbor, Phil Berning, who was one of the best golfers of his era in our home town of Fort Wayne, Indiana. I figured he knew what he was talking about and before too long it became second nature. It has served me well ever since; none of the professionals from whom I have taken lessons have ever thought I needed to change my grip.

A Caveat to the Three Knuckles Visible Grip

The size of your hands may require adjusting the size of the spots to be used in the three knuckles visible technique, and may also require grip adjustments from what I recommend. Golfers with large hands may not see the spot on the third knuckle of the upper hand, or the spot on the second knuckle of the lower hand. Those with small hands may see more than a hint of the spot on the third knuckle of the upper hand, and may not be able to comfortably get the lower hand thumb pad fully into the position I described. Women in particular may have this challenge. Adjust your grip as necessary—the most common adjustment I see golfers make is to rotate the lower hand a bit more

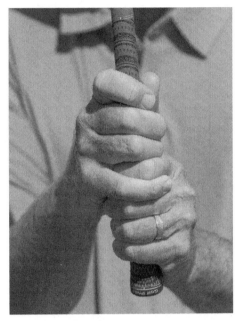

The overlapping grip.

The interlocking, or Vardon, grip.

to the back than a strict use of the technique would require—but do not stray too far from what I have written, and your grip will serve your game well.

Grip Style

The principal variation to the grip I've just described, which is called the overlapping grip, is the interlocking, or Vardon, grip. In the interlocking grip the little finger of the lower hand interlocks with the first finger of the upper hand, instead of resting next to the first finger. The interlocking style is not comfortable to me, but if it is comfortable, use it—as long as you have the other basic parts of the grip correct either one will work. Jack Nicklaus used the Vardon grip; it certainly worked for him.

A third grip style, the baseball grip, is rarely used by good golfers, though is common among weekend golfers. This grip is what the name suggests—the golfer holds the club as he might hold a baseball bat, one hand next to the other, not overlapped or interlocked. The problem with the baseball grip is the lower hand tends to dominate over the upper hand, leading to all sorts of problems. Better to focus on the overlapping or interlocking styles, and watch your game improve accordingly.

You might have read about the hands-parallel nature of the golf grip. I do not think that image is one the average golfer should rely on, except perhaps when putting, which requires a different grip entirely, as I write about in the chapter *Putting*. A good golf grip has one hand slightly over the other, and it is hard for me to visualize how the hands can at the same time be parallel.

Grip Pressure

Never, ever, ever, grip the club too tight. The club needs to be held only firmly enough that no relative motion occurs between the hands and the club at any stage of the swing. The pressure should be in the last three fingers of the upper hand on the club, and the middle two fingers of the lower hand. Work to consciously relax the other fingers and the thumbs—they are just along for the ride.

To maintain control of the club, grip pressure must be firm but not with a high level of tension in the forearm muscles. Those muscles must be ready for action, but in a relaxed manner. Too much lower hand pressure can cause snap hooks, a tendency to pull the ball, or even hard slices, all depending on how the lower hand's pressure acts during the swing. Too much upper hand pressure tends to tighten the muscles in the wrist and forearm, hinders the backswing at the top, and makes the follow-through difficult to carry out.

Grip Strength

The grip described above is neutral-strength, meaning it does not make the golfer tend to hook or to slice. As your game improves, it will be important to know how to bias the grip for special shots, and to do so a good understanding of strong and weak grips is required.

A strong grip means the upper hand has a stronger role in comparison to the lower. This grip helps hook the ball. Take the basic grip as above, but rotate the upper hand slightly backward (e.g. to the right for a right-hander) before overlaying the lower hand. You should now see three black marks on the upper hand, and perhaps the fourth knuckle as well.

A weak grip is the opposite—rotate the upper hand forward so when the lower hand grips the shaft both of the two black marks can be seen. It is possible that only a hint of the black mark on the second knuckle of the upper hand will be visible. This can be called the no finger grip, because the shaft of the club lies at the base of all four fingers, instead of across the lower portion of the first finger. A weak grip tends to make the ball slice.

So remember, more than two knuckles visible on the upper hand is a strong grip. More than one knuckle visible on the lower hand is a weak grip. The ball may not always fly straight, but your game will be off to a better start with a neutral-strength grip.

As years have been added to my calendar of life, I find that I do not completely wrap the lower hand over the upper for every shot, as I recommend, certainly not as much as I used to. I am not sure why I have made the change, it is just a comfort thing that has crept in over the years. I don't move the upper hand to the back, only the lower hand. My grip is still working pretty well, which is the bottom line we all want.

About Long Thumbs, Short Thumbs and That Oily Feeling

Tom Watson has written he prefers the short thumb position for his upper hand. I find the short thumb position helps balance grip pressure between the two hands, a good thing.

Grip the club with the upper hand only. Now increase the pressure, to hold the club tightly. The thumb pad will be more tightly in contact with the fingertips, which are folded around and come up from beneath the shaft of the club. The wrist and forearm muscles will feel more tensed. The sensation will be that the palm of the hand is grasping the club. The thumb will extend farther down along the shaft of the club than it did before the grip pressure was increased—thus a long thumb.

Now reduce the pressure. There will be more of a feeling that the fingers are grasping the club; the palm, first finger, and thumb will be more relaxed. The tension in the wrist and forearm will largely be gone. The thumb pad will only be slightly touching the fingertips, if touching at all. The thumb will not be extended as far down the shaft of the club—thus a short thumb. (In the photos, note the difference in the distances from the thumbnail to the word "Golf.")

Now finish the grip with the lower hand. If the lower hand grips the club too tightly, an increase in the tension in the upper hand results, leading to a loss of the short thumb. The short thumb therefore helps keep the minimum amount of pressure in both hands that is necessary to control of the club. The short thumb also promotes a looser, lighter feeling in the hands, which in part is "that oily feeling" that Sam Snead always said he wanted in all parts of his swing. His "oily feeling" is important to be able to complete a full turn at the top of the swing. It also helps maintain flexibility in the hands, wrists, and forearms, and promotes good action through the ball when the club is in the hitting area.

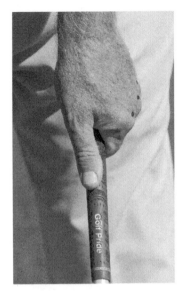

The long thumb.

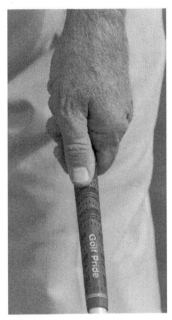

The short thumb.

Mulligan

Don't Strangle the Grip

We have all seen it: the golfer at the tee holding the club so tight the muscles and veins in his forearms are taught and distended. We have probably also all seen the resulting shot is almost never a success.

Tension does not work in golf. Mental tension does not work. Physical tension does not work. Relaxation is a key to success in this game. It must start with relaxation in the hands and forearms.

The waggle.

The takeaway.

The Basics

The Waggle and the Takeaway

Television golf viewers frequently focus on how far past vertical the best golfers get at the top of their backswings. They would be better served by studying everything that has to happen before the club gets to the top. For example, consider the "waggle" and the "takeaway"—what they are, how they differ, and why they are both important.

The waggle is a relaxed, loose-muscled movement of the clubhead occurring when a golfer is preparing to hit the ball, but before the swing starts. It is done with the club off the ground, and is solely a movement of the wrists and hands. To waggle the clubhead means to repeatedly flex the wrists without moving the arms. The flexing moves the clubhead backward, then forward, but is not a repetition of the start of the swing because the wrists are not flexed at the beginning of the swing. The waggle is intended to prevent the hands, wrists, and forearms from tensing up before the swing starts—tension otherwise constraining the swing and reducing the distance the ball flies. Some instructors say to never waggle the club because it might increase the possibility of incorrectly starting the swing with that same wrist and hand movement. Starting the swing incorrectly with a waggle is a reasonable concern, and a problem to work to avoid, but the tension-reducing effect of the waggle is important and I think more golfers should use it in their swing preparation.

The takeaway is the opposite of the waggle—it is the start of the swing. It is done with the club off the ground, and is a movement of the arms, wrists, and hands in unison, with the shoulders following quickly thereafter. It is not a flexing of the wrists and hands, rather is the structured sequence that is the start of the swing. A proper takeaway is essential if the important distance-producing body movements—the shoulder turn and weight shift—are to occur correctly.

Ricky Fowler is an example of a tour pro who prepares for his swing with several repeated practice takeaways. Some golfers, including Ricky, occasionally prepare to hit the ball by extending the takeaway into a partial full swing several times before hitting the ball. Justin Leonard frequently did this, as did Mike Weir, the Canadian left hander. Not many golfers use either repetitions of the takeaway or half swings in preparing for hitting the ball, but if you are comfortable, by all means go ahead. Just be sure the half swing starts with a takeaway, not a waggle.

Mulligan

Old Dogs Can Learn New Tricks

Back a few pages, in the chapter titled *The Grip*, I wrote that the interlocking grip did not work for me, it was not comfortable. Surprise, surprise. Turns out not to be true.

My recent driving range practice has been focused on improving the repeatability of the position of the club at the top of the backswing. Swing repeatability cannot be attained if the hands are not in the correct position throughout the swing, but at the same time I have always known the palm of my lower hand often loses contact with the club at the top of my backswing. The club cannot be in a repeatable position at the top if the hand-to-club position changes during the swing.

Shortly before this book went to press, it came to my mind to change from the overlapping to the interlocking grip to see what the result might be. Not surprisingly, the interlocking grip helps ensure the lower hand stays better positioned on the club throughout the swing.

The interlocking grip feels different than I am used to—I used the overlapping grip for decades—but if the result is improvement in my backswing club position I will certainly continue to use it. This old dog is trying to learn a new trick.

To improve our golf games, we cannot continue to do the same things we have always done just because we have always done them. Perhaps the tour professionals can, but not the rest of us. Take time to evaluate the weaknesses in every aspect of your game. Work focused on eliminating those weaknesses will soon be reflected on your scorecards.

The Basics

Stance and Weight Distribution

Here is a clothing optional test to help you determine which stance is best for your body style—the standard professional or the modified professional. Stand in front of a mirror with both feet close together and pointing straight ahead. If your knees also point straight ahead, congratulations, you can use the standard professional stance. If your knees point inward—are not in line with your feet—you need the modified professional stance. This probably means you are a bit bowlegged. That doesn't make any difference to your golf game, as long as you use the modified professional stance. So don't go into counseling or anything.

The Standard Professional Stance

Stand with your feet shoulder-width apart. Point the back foot straight ahead, or perhaps slightly backwards if doing so is more comfortable. Turn the forward foot toward the target, fifteen or twenty degrees from straight ahead. That is it—go ahead and adjust your stance to get comfortable, but don't stray too far from this standard.

The Modified Professional Stance

This stance requires the golfer to line up the knees instead of the feet. Turn the back foot backwards enough to get the back knee pointed about straight forward, or perhaps slightly to the back, again, the goal is to be comfortable. Turn the forward foot toward the target enough to get the forward knee pointed about ten or fifteen degrees toward the target. Your forward foot will point more forward than the knee does. Don't stray too far from this standard, but go ahead and adjust the modified professional stance to your own comfort level.

A good stance ensures the body's characteristics do not constrain the swing's lower body movements. With either stance, distance and directional control problems result if the feet and knees are turned too far one way or the other. The swing constraints that often come with age, and the associated loss of flexibility, may be reduced or eliminated if both feet are turned more outward. Older golfers also tend to move their feet closer together than when they were younger. All of this is fine. More than anything else, golfers must be comfortable when addressing the ball.

In the second paragraph I said to stand "with your feet shoulder width apart." Be realistic—many golfers stand with their feet too far apart. Test the width of your stance by addressing the ball with the feet pointed straight ahead. Hold a club from a point in front of one shoulder and see if the club hangs directly over that foot. Do the same thing with the other shoulder and foot. Do not be surprised if this test leads you to bring your feet closer together.

Weight Distribution in the Stance

The body's weight distribution in the stance will change from club to club and from shot to shot. The paragraphs in this chapter focus on the long clubs; later chapters will cover this subject for the short game.

When addressing the ball with the long clubs, the usual guidance is to have the weight about evenly distributed from side-to-side. True enough, but read on—I will return for more words on this truth in a few paragraphs.

Most golfers find an inside-of-the-foot weight bias helps maintain a light feeling in the stance, and prevents too much tension from building up in the legs. It also helps maintain flexibility in the lower body, which in turn helps retain a proper balance during the swing. So work to keep your body weight biased to the inside of each foot.

If the stance and weight distribution were only that easy, we could move on. But they aren't.

You may have heard the phrase "a good stance will make you feel like you are about to take a step down the fairway," or as if "you are leaning down the fairway." Let me explain the cause of that feeling.

For right-handed golfers, because the right hand is on the club below the left hand, the right shoulder will be slightly below the left shoulder when addressing the ball. For that reason, the inner ear—where balance comes from—will want more weight to be on the right foot. But I said the usual guidance is for the weight is to be evenly distributed from side-to-side. The inner ear as a result essentially concludes that weight is being shifted from right to left, leading to the feeling "you are about to take a step down the fairway."

Now more about the truth "your weight should be about evenly distributed from side-to-side." If you have watched the pros on TV, you will know how dramatically they finish their swings, with hands high in the air and the body balanced nearly entirely on the forward foot. We amateurs often do not finish our swings that well—we do not get our weight on the forward side as well as we should, thus losing both distance and consistency. But how to cure this problem?

What I have been doing in recent years is to start my stance with more weight on my forward side—not evenly distributed between my feet but biased slightly forward. That helps me complete my swing better, especially with my long clubs. We will return to the topic of weight distribution when we talk about the mechanics of the backswing and the downswing, but if starting with more weight on the forward foot helps your finish then by all means go for it.

As with the grip, the proper stance may create an unnatural feeling, and will take time to adjust to. A good stance, as with a correct grip, is essential to good golf, so put range work in using the stance I have just described. Your game will respond accordingly.

Mulligan

Where and When to Give and Receive Golf Tips

During a weekend break from a two week training course I attended a number of years ago several of us went out to play golf on Saturday and Sunday. Solely casual games. We all played about our usual games, some holes good, some bad. Good fun was being had by all.

Near the end of the Sunday round, however, a member of my foursome, who had been getting increasingly frustrated with his game, made a comment along the lines of "Somebody please tell me what I am doing wrong!"

It is usually a mistake to do so, but I took the bait and suggested he narrow his stance. I knew him from past business but we had never played golf together, and had noticed his stance was much too wide. Four or more inches too wide.

There were only three holes remaining and for the rest of the round he hit every shot better than he had hit anything that weekend. He was quite appreciative. Tips usually do not work out so well but it felt good to help out a friend.

The message here? First, some parts of the game can be fixed quickly with immediate results, others cannot. Second, there are parts of the golf game we can correct ourselves—the grip for example. Other parts we cannot see quite so clearly. Listen to those in the know about golf, even in a casual round if need be. It is always better to learn on the range, but occasionally changes on the course in real time can work out as well.

The Basics

Ball Position

Ball position is another aspect of golf in which recommendations have changed over the years. When I first started playing, I was told that, for the driver, the ball should be just inside my forward heel, teed moderately high. For each increasingly more lofted club, I was to move the ball farther back in my stance. Continuing through the clubs in the bag meant the ball was just inside my back heel for the pitching wedge. I followed this guidance for decades, but it is not considered best practice today.

For the driver, the ball should be teed relatively high, with half to two-thirds of the ball extending above the top of the driver (some better golfers have it even higher). Technology has a lot to do with this change. The sweet spot for metal-headed drivers is considered to require a higher teed ball. The ball, though, is still intended to be swept off the tee in an upward movement of the club, thus the more forward positioning of the ball. All this together ensures the sweet spot of the club and the ball perfectly match in that sweeping action.

Modern guidance for the driver is for the ball to be directly in front of the forward toe—if the foot was pointed straight forward. Since that toe points somewhat toward the target however, as described in the last chapter, I have the ball directly in front of the arch of my forward foot. You might prefer to have the ball directly in front of the forward heel, though most better golfers do not have it any farther back.

If you have not been using this ball position or tee height, both will take time to get used to. I find the forward ball position makes it hard to get my alignment correct, and alignment is a frequent driving range focus point for me. I have also had to adjust to teeing the ball up this high.

When teeing off with a higher-lofted metal-headed club, the ball will need to be farther back in the stance, and not teed up quite as high. Personal preference comes into play here—what works best for you may not be what works best for me—but do not move the ball too far back from the forward heel.

With hybrids, the ball should be positioned the same as for higher-lofted metals, or slightly farther back. Most golfers move the ball a bit farther back for hybrid tee shots, but again, there is some personal preference involved here. The ball will need to be teed closer to the ground.

Ball position in the fairway is different. For both metals and hybrids, the ball will be at least two to three inches inside the forward heel. Some golfers have the ball as far back as the center of the stance.

My ball position recommendation for irons changes for each club. For the longest iron club I carry, which today is a four iron, I have my standard, full width, stance. The ball is about four inches inside my forward heel, which makes it a bit more than that from my back heel. (The distance from the forward heel is not absolute; within reason, every golfer needs to adapt to his or her own comfort level.) For each increasingly higher lofted club, I move my back foot forward enough to be comfortable with the shorter club, but keep the ball in the same position relative to my forward foot.

The approach I recommend for irons is better than prior guidance because the balance in the stance adjusts automatically for each club. The back foot's forward movement forces a forward shift in the body's weight distribution, which is what is needed for higher lofted clubs, thus giving one less thing to think about in preparing for the swing.

Mulligan

Make Sure Your Strategic Decisions Fit the Hole

Long before the age of the internet, newspapers published cartoon-sketch articles giving tips on the golf game. The first I remember was by Arnold Palmer; later on both Jack Nicklaus and Gary Player had similar series.

I particularly recall one from the late 1960s by Gary Player. The message was to always think about which side of the teeing area to hit from. He wrote that if the trouble on the hole was on the left, we should not tee off from the right, as by doing so we would be aiming toward the left side. Instead, he told us to tee off from the left side and point the other direction.

This simple strategic tip is well understood by most golfers, but is also often misapplied. Here is an example of when not to follow Player's tip. At my home course the ninth hole is a medium length, par five, a really good hole. The tee shot is over a ravine/waste area; just after the landing area the direction of the fairway shifts to the left at an angle of twenty or thirty degrees. There are heavily wooded areas on both sides of the fairway, but because the fairway has a landing area bulging out to the right, golfers commonly tee off on the left side of the teeing area. I did as well for a long time.

The problem with teeing off on the left side of the tee is that a good drive often runs too far to the right. Although there is plenty of room in the fairway for the second shot, the fairway turns back to the right about where the second shot landing area is. If the tee shot is to the right, the ideal ball flight for the second shot is constrained by tall trees on the right, making it harder to ideally place the second shot, thus limiting the possibility that the third shot, which is over water to the green, can attack the pin.

The ninth hole at Grand Pines Golf Club.
Montgomery Texas, © 2017 Google.
The tee is on the left; the line in the direction of the right
side of the fairway is from the left side of the tee.

For this well designed hole, the better strategic decision is to tee off from the right, or at most center-right, of the tee and work the ball along the left side of the fairway, with a slight draw if possible. The resulting left-center tee shot location is ideal to place the second shot in the landing area, which by-the-way runs downhill towards a creek, leaving a wedge to the pin and a putt for a birdie.

Strategy is an important component of good golf, but make sure your strategy fits every aspect of the holes you play.

The Basics

The Rest of the Stance

If the feet are positioned, and the weight distributed, correctly, the rest of the stance falls into place rather easily.

Both knees should be slightly bent—the standard phrase is "just as if you were about to sit down." I bend my knees a bit and make sure they are loose and comfortable; the standard phrase does not help me much. I also think about getting my knees almost to the point of being over the balls of my feet, though in truth they probably are nearer being over the arches of my feet.

Your back will be almost straight but not stiff. It will not be straight up, of course, since you have to lean to address the ball, thus it will be forward from vertical.

Your rear end should stick out a bit. It will stick out more if you have a big rear end.

Your shoulders should hang down and be slightly rounded. Not stiff as if you are at attention. Not soldierly.

Your head needs to point upward above a line that would be an extension of your spine. It needs to be above that line so your chin will be up and out of the way of the forward shoulder during the backswing. We will return to this thought more in later chapters—it is a subtle stance requirement that is not often talked about. If you wear glasses, as I do, address the ball by looking out of the bottom one-third of your lens, perhaps biased to looking at the ball more out of the back eye. This bias ensures your head will be pointed up and turned towards the fairway, and thus automatically in the correct position.

Address, front view with driver.

Address, side view with driver.

Address, side view with seven iron.

Your arms and hands will hang down naturally from the shoulders, with about a fist's width distance between the crotch and the hands. If your hands are too close to your body, you won't be able to turn very well or get the club on the proper swing plane. If your hands are too far from your body, you will be able to turn but you won't be able to control your swing, your weight transfer during your swing, or your follow-through. A fair number of tour professionals have their hands farther from their bodies than I recommend, but to do so I find takes a good amount of practice to get both comfortable and consistent.

You need to feel light on your feet. A phrase I have heard is "it's better if you feel almost as if someone could push you over, forward or backward, with a light tap." In my swing preparation I rock back and forth both from left to right and from front to back before I start my backswing. This helps me keep light and loose, and prevents tension from building up before the swing starts.

Mulligan

No Crabbing

As you get settled over the ball, and perhaps are moving your weight back and forth to get comfortable, take care not to unconsciously change the direction of your stance. An easy thing to do is to subtly shift the direction of your feet away from the target line, in a move not unlike how crabs walk themselves down a beach, first to the right, then to the left... Avoid this by only shifting your weight, not lifting your feet off the ground,

The old phrase that golf is a game of inches is true, but it is also a game of tenths of inches. Don't let a few tenths in your stance get in the way of hitting the ball straight down the fairway.

The Basics

The Pre-Shot Routine

Repeatability is the key to good, consistent golf. A mechanical, pre-shot routine is an essential part of that consistency. Here is my routine, all of which is second nature, the result of decades of finding what works for me. Think about each step, adapt it to your own style, and your best golf will come in much less than the decades it has taken me.

1. Look over the teeing ground. Find a flat area where your feet and the tee will both be on the same level. Most golfers skip this step, but I don't because un-level teeing areas can cause draws or fades, and psychologically give me bad vibes.

2. Make sure the height of the ball on the tee is correct for the club and the shot you plan to make. From behind the ball, look down the fairway and pick a target towards which you want to hit the ball. Draw an imaginary line from the target back to the ball, look one to three feet in front of your ball and find a spot on the line. The spot may be a leaf, an off-colored blade of grass, a divot, or a broken tee. Memorize whatever it is—you will use it to line up your clubface with your target line.

3. While standing behind the ball, place the club on the ground and set your grip. Make sure the club is resting naturally on the ground.

4. Address the ball. With your feet close together, put the club behind the ball. Use the memorized spot to position the clubhead along the target line. Check your grip and the tension in your hands.

5. Set your stance. Many articles say to move the back foot first, then move the forward foot into place. I do the reverse. It seems more comfortable to me, and above all golf is a sport in which a comfortable

feeling goes a long way towards good swings. Once I have each foot in place, I rock from right to left a few times, each time almost but not lifting either foot off the ground. My main purpose is to get comfortable, but there is a second, more important reason. It is easy, when placing the club behind the ball, gripping the club, and putting the feet into place, to unconsciously develop an improper weight distribution. These lateral movements help ensure my weight distribution is correct, and my weight is on the inside of each foot. I don't focus on repositioning my weight, but I know that is what the side to side movements do.

6. Next get the legs and knees in a proper orientation. I flex my knees as if I were about to do a deep knee bend, or to sit down on a high stool, but of course move only slightly downward. At the same time, I also rock front to rear to make sure my weight distribution is not biased either to the balls of my feet or to my heels. I work to ensure my weight is centered over the arches of my feet. Find your comfort level, but do not let your weight go too far in either direction. The purpose of this step is to keep the legs and lower body relaxed and ready to start the swing, and to get the proper front-to-back weight distribution. A smooth full swing is impossible if the legs and knees are stiff, or if your weight is overly biased one way or the other.

7. This is a good time to check key points from earlier chapters. Make sure your back is correctly set and not stiff. A line through your spine will lean slightly forward toward the ball. Check to ensure your hands are properly spaced away from your body.

8. The last step is to check your head position. For a long time I rotated my head backwards, ten or fifteen degrees or so. I now think it is much better to rotate the head forward, by about the same amount, almost as if looking down the fairway at address. That position makes it easier to maintain a motionless head until late in the swing. A second key is to have the head up so the forward shoulder can move under the chin during the backswing. I know my head angle is correct if I feel like I am looking out of the bottom right portion of the lenses in my glasses.

9. Finally, check shoulder positions—the back shoulder will be lower than the forward, with both arms hanging freely downwards. Your arms should be rotated slightly inward, so each elbow is pointing to its respective hip. I have a tendency to let my back arm and elbow be too relaxed, and have to focus on rotating the back elbow inward, so that it points more toward my body. Doing so helps me maintain a better position of that arm during the backswing. I said in the grip chapter I didn't think the parallel hands view of the grip was something the average golfer should use. However, if the elbows are correctly positioned, the forearms will face each other, not parallel because each arm extends upwards towards its respective shoulder, but otherwise facing each other. That idea works better for me than does the parallel hands thought.

Don't be afraid to stop and start over again if at any time you don't feel comfortable. The most common problems are the ball is teed at the wrong height, or the stance is not correctly lined up with the target line. Repeating this procedure often enough will make your game consistent, and you will quickly do all of the above steps as second nature.

Those who have played a lot of golf before reading this book know this chapter includes a lot of detail for a part of the game preferably requiring only a few seconds. The best thing a golfer can do is make this routine an automatic habit; no conscious thought needed. That's why it is essential to follow the same routine on the driving range—practice on the range is invaluable for making the pre-shot routine a part of hitting every shot well in every round you play.

Mulligan

These Guys Are Good

That is the sum total of *The Basics* of the golf game. What I have written is not difficult, and we can all, with a little work, get ourselves set up with the correct grip, stance, weight distribution, and preparation routine. The golf swing itself is a lot harder to carry out than these basic topics.

Just as it is harder to carry out, the next part—*The Swing*—is harder to write about. All golfers, if they are serious about improving, need to do more than merely go play a few times a month. Go to the range. Go to the putting green (or put an old carpet in your garage and practice putting at home). Read books. But there are two other things golfers should be doing.

First, watching golf on television. In particular, watch LPGA tournaments. Why LPGA? Simple. We are more like them than we are like the men on the PGA Tour.

Look at Tiger when he was in his prime. Look at Dustin Johnson, Jason Day, Bubba Watson, Phil Mickelson, and the others near the top of the leaderboard week in and week out. They can all do things with their swings we cannot do. Do not let yourself believe that because someone like Phil does not have the build of a Tiger or a Dustin he does not have the muscle strength and tone to do what he needs to do with the club and the ball. Most of us do not come close to having the muscle strength and tone the men on the PGA Tour have.

We also do not likely have the muscle tone LPGA professionals have. The difference though, as compared to the men, is women do not generally have the same inherent level of strength men have. So how do the women perform at such a high level? They do so by mastering all the details of the golf swing. They do not often try to overpower the ball, as the men do, they more often finesse the ball. In a sense, they have swings similar to the swings of golfers in days gone by, before technology allowed so much more to be done with the club and the ball.

Because the women do not often try to overpower the ball, we can learn more by watching them than we can learn from the men. Think of Annika Sorenstam in her prime. Her tempo was perfect, her swing plane was perfect, her rhythm was perfect, and she always smoothly swung through the ball and ended up in the perfect follow-through position—weight on the forward foot, balanced by the back foot. I always thought, while watching Annika swing, "I should be able to swing like." She made it look easy. The men do not usually make it look easy. They just look very, very impressive.

The second thing golfers should do is get lessons from their local pros. Reading books like this one, and practicing what is written, can get a handicap down into the low teens, perhaps lower. But to get a low handicap, we need an expert's guidance to know what to work on. Get a lesson from your PGA professional. Those guys really are good.

Forward press.

The Swing

Starting the Swing

I start my swing with a forward press, though much less of one than I used to have. The forward press is an old-school move not taught much anymore, but if you watch films from the golden age of TV golf—the 1960s when only the last four or five holes of tournaments were televised and when it was common to have televised one-on-one competitions such as *Shell's Wonderful World of Golf*—you will see quite a number of the best pros in years past had a forward press as part of their swing. Golfers today are usually taught not to start with a forward press—a mistake in my opinion. The golf swing is an unnatural motion in some ways, and particularly so if it starts from a motionless position. I find it hard to maintain the relaxed but ready for action tension that should be in the hands and arms if the swing starts from a fully motionless position. It is also hard to maintain a smooth rhythm if the swing is started from a dead stop.

My forward press is a simple motion—just a slight press forward, down the target line, of my back knee, with the rest of the back leg moving very little. It is not a big move, and over the years has become smaller. At the same time, my weight shifts slightly to the inside of my forward foot. As I have gotten older the weight shift part of my forward press has become almost nonexistent. All this removes any last bit of tension that may have crept into my muscles during my setup routine, and leads to a nice, smooth takeaway.

The forward press is easy to overdo, perhaps the reason it is not taught as much as it once was. I used to also move my hips forward, and even sometimes my shoulders. Those motions can lead to a tendency to open up the hips too much in the downswing, which can lead to pulling or slicing the ball and losing power. Limit your forward press to the back knee, and perhaps the leg, and you'll be better off.

At the end of the forward press, the swing should start smoothly. Except for the return of the back knee to its starting position, the body's motions in the takeaway are all in the arms and shoulders. Those motions are a simple rotation around a pivot point at the lower part of the neck; nothing else moves during the start of the swing.

The forearms move in line with the hands during the takeaway; the wrists do not cock yet. If the rotation in the arms and shoulders is correct, and the wrists do not get involved too early, the swing will continue with the clubhead pointing along an extension of the target line back from the ball. Pointing the clubhead along that line ensures a maximum swing arc, which is important to hit the ball hard. Amateurs frequently bring the clubhead inside the backward extension of the target line too soon, with the typical result of weak drives which fade or slice.

The swing's rhythm will be better if the rest of the body is not moving during the takeaway. Golfers too often do too many things too early in the swing, when they should only be rotating their arms and shoulders. Doing so is a good way to kill the rhythm needed for swing repeatability.

This stage of the swing ends when the wrists begin to cock, a point which varies greatly among the best golfers. Don't over worry the point at which your wrists begin to cock—it has to be natural for you and your swing mechanics. Greg Norman had a late wrist cock, while Nick Faldo and Tom Watson cocked their wrists early in the swing. I would take any of those swings. Just be comfortable in your transition from the rotation involved in the takeaway to the continuation of the swing.

Don't overwork the start of the swing if a forward press is not comfortable. But if you are one of those golfers who gets a lot of tension built up when are addressing the ball, it may be something to try.

Mulligan

So, What Does "Keep Your Head Down" Mean Anyway?

Even non-golfers have heard these common golf course phrases:

"I looked up."

"I moved my head,"

"Keep your head down."

And the list goes on. But what do these phrases mean? Do they in fact mean anything at all?

I am not sure I know what they mean, and I am not sure they mean what the average golfer thinks they mean. But I am sure most are focusing on the wrong thing when they use those phrases, or at least are focusing on something not likely to help their games all that much.

I keep the phrase "I want the whites of my eyes on the white of the ball" in my mind when I am practicing and playing. When I am addressing the ball, I focus my eyes like a laser on the white portion at the back of the ball I want the clubhead to contact. I do not let my eyes move from looking in that direction until the ball is long gone.

The whites of my eyes thought works for me because I know what it means, and I know what good it does for my golf swing. First, during the backswing, the laser focus ensures that my eyes, and thus my head, remain in position, and this in turn ensures my shoulders rotate underneath my head, as they should. Second, during the downswing up to and through contact, that laser focus ensures the reverse happens—the eyes and head stay in position as the lower body is turning forward, as the shoulders and hips are unwinding and as the arms are bringing the club down toward the ball. Third, and finally, the laser focus means by the time my swing has reached the follow-through, my eyes and head can do nothing bad to disrupt my swing mechanics.

Two messages here. First, if you are going to use a phrase to help you improve your golf game, make sure you know what it means. Second, focus the whites of your eyes on the white of the ball. It really does work.

The Swing

Arm Action in the Backswing

A golfer's preparations for the full swing end with the forward press and the takeaway. Those preparations also end the "easy" parts of the swing, both to describe and to understand. Let's philosophize about what has to happen in the backswing before getting into the actual movements that golfers must make to successfully carry out a full swing shot.

The Forward Arm (left for right-handers, right for left-handers)

We don't need to spend a lot of time on the forward arm in the backswing:

1)   If straight and unflexed, it provides the longest possible length for the arc of your swing, and

2)   If straight and unflexed, it facilitates the maximum transmission of rotational energy to the clubhead.

These points are essential to understand for a golfer to consistently hit the ball. Keep in mind, however, the forward arm should not be rigid, and the elbow not locked stiff, because to do either limits the ability to fully turn the upper body. Instead, the arm and elbow are preferably straight and unflexed, but not tensed to the point where the arm muscles constrain the shoulder turn.

A straight forward arm provides repeatability to the swing, because it is an easy position to maintain. Repeatability means swing control and consistency. Work to keep the arm extended and straight, but not rigid, and use it to help your shoulders fully turn.

The Back Arm (right for right-handers, left for left-handers)

The back arm and elbow have dual roles in the backswing. They provide something of a "second nature" guide for the look and feel of the backswing, and also provide a mechanism for imparting power from the back side of the body to the ball.

To understand these dual roles, think back to the start of the swing. The straight forward arm keeps the clubhead pointing along an extension of the target line to the rear of the tee. At first, the back arm is also fully extended. As the swing continues, the turn of the shoulders draws the club up along the backward extension of the target line. The swing plane is angled upward and toward the back, intersecting the target line. At this point something has to give—you can't continue the swing along that plane with both arms extended and at the same maintain the stance and lower body position we want.

That is why I think the "look and feel" guide the back arm provides to the swing is so important. The key to the swing plane is in the back arm and elbow's action in the backswing (Not to mention wrist action, which is discussed in the next chapter). When the clubhead starts to move up and away from the target line extension, the back elbow bends and folds inward towards the body. The bend and fold enables the arms and shoulders to elevate the clubhead along the swing plane to the top of the backswing.

Properly positioning the back arm's elbow requires more work than most golfers realize. The elbow should not be unnaturally close to, nor far from, the body. At the top of the backswing the elbow should point neither down nor upward. Instead, the upper arm should be about parallel to the ground, with the elbow pointing about horizontally to the back. If you get to this position at the top of the backswing, your swing has likely followed the correct swing plane.

Proper positioning of the back arm and elbow is important for both control and distance. The farther from the body the arm and elbow move at the top of the swing, the more likely it is the wrists and forearms also move away from the proper swing plane. The clubhead then becomes harder to control at the top of the swing, which leads to directional control inconsistency. On the other hand, an arm and elbow cramped next to the body makes it more difficult to develop the full power the swing needs, meaning loss of distance. Think about the different roles of each arm, and work to get both into the position maximizing your ability to control the ball and hit it far.

Mulligan

Is There a Secret to Hitting the Ball Really Far?

We have all seen, on television or in person, a golfer who seems to swing effortlessly yet gets long distances with all of his or her clubs. The best example on the PGA Tour has long been Fred Couples, who never looks like he is swinging hard. LPGA Hall of Fame member Laura Davies also hits the ball far, but seems to be swinging harder than does Couples. Why do these swings look so different? What similarities do they have that so reliably give them both such long distances?

The answer to those questions are why the last chapter *Arm Action in the Backswing*, the next chapter *The Wrists and Forearms in the Backswing*, and a chapter yet to come, *Swinging Through the Ball*, are all so important.

The golf swing attributes that Fred Couples and Laura Davies have in common are their masterful arm positions and wrist cocking in the backswing, and their equally, or more, masterful arm positioning and wrist uncocking at ball contact. Distance for a driver or any other club in the bag comes from those actions. The fact that Couples looks to be applying less force than does Davies is not really the key point; neither would hit the ball far without mastering the use of their arms and wrists, not to mention the other golf swing characteristics this book discusses.

A friend of mine has a swing much like Fred Couples—smooth, relaxed, with not really much force being visibly applied. In contrast, my swing is more like Laura Davies, with much more force seeming to be applied. The difference between us is that I have not mastered my wrist action as well as my friend has. As I have said elsewhere, I do not have ideal wrist and arm action in my swing, and as a result have always looked like I am applying force to the ball with more use of my shoulders and upper body than does my friend. (Not a bad thing necessarily, but not ideal either.)

To answer the question posed in the title of this *Mulligan* "No, there is no secret." Study the three chapters I listed in the second paragraph above and work to master the techniques they discuss. Your golf game will be the better for it.

The Wrists and Forearms in the Backswing

This is without a doubt the hardest chapter for me to write. It is the hardest subject to understand from a technical analysis of the golf swing point of view. It is the hardest subject for amateurs to get right. It is one of the hardest subjects for amateurs to figure out whether they are getting it right. It may well be the hardest part of the golf swing for an amateur to know whether he should even wonder whether or not he is getting it right. Does that make it hard enough for you?

I have always thought I had weak wrist and forearm action, at least in part because I knew my high ball flight was not what pros get when we watch them play. Even though there are many differences between the pros and golfers like me, I had a feeling something was not quite right. But more to the point, I did not really know what I meant when I said to myself I had "weak wrist and forearm action."

For a long time I did not think or worry about it—largely because I grew up on a par three course and was always able to find a way to get my irons to work more or less as intended. But if I had one wish about my golf game, it would be to go back in time and correct the weaknesses in my wrist and forearm action when I was much younger. Even though I know what I need to do—at least I think I do—poor wrist and forearm action is a hard thing to correct late in life.

If you have watched slow motion repetitions of any professional golfer's swing, and listened to the announcer's analysis, you will know the swing characteristic giving them distance, control, and power is their wrist and forearm action. Think about it this way: At address, the arms extend down and forward from the shoulders to the club, and the club extends down and forward from the arms to the ball. Although I haven't talked about the downswing, the address position is essentially repeated at the moment the club hits the ball. In between, though, at the top of the backswing, the arms make nearly a right angle with the club. The extra power we see when the pros hit the ball comes from the way they transition from the address position, when the forearms and wrists are uncocked, to the top of the swing, when the forearms and wrists are fully cocked, and then back to an uncocked position at ball contact, which is the "release" we often hear or read about.

Two things have to happen between address and the top of the swing. First, the forearms have to rotate, and second, the wrists have to get fully cocked. These two actions are not entirely independent, but to ensure a full understanding of this important subject the next paragraphs will cover both actions as if they were.

Stand as if you were addressing the ball, but without a club. Put your hands together, palms facing each other. Start your backswing with your hands together. Only go back until the forward arm is extended backward parallel to the ground. Your back elbow will have folded up against the body. Your forearms should have rotated so the back of your forward hand faces straight to the front, which is essential to developing a proper backswing. This may seem like a simple drill, but amateur golfers often pick the club up too quickly from address and do not get proper rotation in the forearms.

Wrist cocking in the backswing is more difficult to describe. Let's start with making sure we understand what it means when we say "wrist cocking," because it is different for each wrist. Stand again in a normal position and extend both arms directly forward, with the backs of both hands pointed upward. Start with the back wrist (right for right-handers). Bend it upwards toward the top of that forearm so the back of the hand—if you can (I can't)— makes a 90 degree angle with the upward facing portion of the forearm. This position, when repeated at the top of the backswing, is what is meant by having the back wrist fully cocked.

Now the forward wrist. Start from the same arms to the front, backs of the hands pointed upward, position. Instead of bending the forward wrist upward,

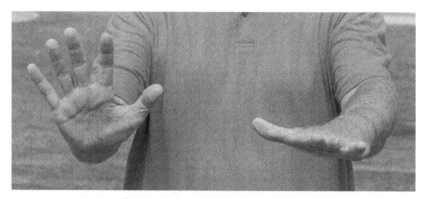

Demonstrating cocked wrist positions.

Mid-backswing wrist and forearm positions.

bend it as far to the back (to the right for right-handers) as you can, again without moving the forearm, to make an angle between your wrist and the backward facing portion of the forearm. This position is what fully cocked means for the forward wrist at the top of the backswing.

If you do both of these at once, while in the arms forward standing-in-place position, it may seem hard to believe they represent the position the arms and wrists should be in at the top of the backswing. But with a little practice, and thought, you will quickly understand they are the best position for your wrists and arms at the top of the golf swing.

Let's put this all together. Take a club and stand ready for a swing. We will consider three swing positions—addressing the ball, the forward arm pointing directly backward, and the top of the backswing.

At address both wrists are fully uncocked. When we move the club back to the forward arm pointed horizontally backward position, the forward wrist is still fully uncocked, but the back wrist has begun to bend in the direction of being, but is not yet, fully cocked. As we continue to the top of the backswing, both wrists will be fully cocked; there should be a straight line from your forward elbow towards and all the way through the forward wrist to the back of the hand.

This last point is important and one I only recently realized was one of my problems. The forward wrist should not allow the hand to bend towards the top of the forward forearm. This position, sometimes referred to as "forward wrist cupping," makes it hard to consistently hit the ball solid and straight.

On the other hand, the position of the back wrist towards the back forearm is a preferable "cupped" position, and something to be worked towards, not to be avoided.

Now let's consider what the professionals do and see how to put all this together in our golf swings. Get a club and stop the backswing when the forward forearm is parallel to the ground. If you have not cocked either wrist, the club will be pointing out to the back. A number of successful pros have this position in their backswings, Vijay Singh, Davis Love, Greg Norman, and Tiger Woods, for example, but I am not sure I recommend it for the average golfer. It is difficult to complete the backswing from this position; the wrist cocking action must be completed during the last half of the backswing at the same time the club is moving into position at the top. Thus the "uncocked at horizontal position" may be more of a challenge than most amateurs should take on. Another reason to avoid this position is the tendency of a late wrist cock to lead to an early wrist uncock in the downswing. At least it has done so for me. In other words, the wrists tend to want to uncock at roughly the same point in the downswing at which they were cocked. But because maximum power is imparted to the ball with a late downswing wrist uncock, it is better if we start to cock our wrists at or before the arm horizontal position.

To practice the preferred wrist action in the backswing, repeat the forearm rotation exercise with the club in hand, but this time start to cock your wrists before your forward forearm reaches the parallel to the ground position. The wrists should not rotate or flex backward or sideways. If you look at the forward hand, you will see an angle between the wrist and the thumb, but you should not see an angle between the wrist and either the back or the palm side of the hand. A sure way to lose power and control is to have the forward wrist break either forward or backward at this point in the swing, so concentrate on having an upward wrist cock in this position.

Top of backswing cocked wrists.

Some golfers, very few I think, can actually bend their forward wrist towards the inside of the forward forearm at the top of their backswing. Dustin Johnson has an amazing swing for many reasons, and is one golfer who can do this. Look for pictures of him at the top of his backswing and focus on his hand position and wrist cock. An amazing swing.

Summarizing what I recommend, at the forward arm horizontal to the ground point in the backswing, the club will be pointing at least partially upward, and for some golfers at a nearly ninety degree angle from the arm. If the forearms have been rotated properly, the bottom part of the back of the forward hand, i.e. the portion of the hand just below the little finger, will face slightly forward, and the back of the hand will be angled upward and slightly to the rear. At this point the back wrist will be slightly, but not fully, cocked, at least not for most of us.

The timing of the wrist cock is golfer-specific. For some golfers, both wrists will be fully cocked at this position and from this point until the top of the backswing there will be no further relative motion between the wrists and forearms. The raising of the forward arm and the turn of the shoulders and the hips are the principal motions getting the club to the top of the backswing. This "nearly ninety degree wrist angle at horizontal" is the wrist action Tom Watson and Nick Faldo used, and that's good enough for me. If your wrists are not fully cocked at this position, no worries, just be sure they cock before your backswing is finished.

In addition to being a key factor in developing maximum power at the downswing release point, proper wrist cock action helps keep the backswing on the proper swing plane. Flexing the wrists incorrectly may lead to bringing the club inside too soon, a fault which will in turn need to be corrected at the top to get the downswing moving along the proper plane for contact with the ball. So, if you see the bottom edge of the forward hand is pointing more than merely a bit forward, then you have flexed the wrist backward or have moved the club inside too soon, or both.

Do not try to have the same wrist cock timing for every club in your bag. As I write in other chapters, you should cock your wrists earlier with your short irons, because you are not trying for maximum distance with those clubs but rather are trying for ball control at a target distance. On the other hand, with your long irons and woods you may need to slightly delay your wrist cock because the club is longer and has a larger, heavier head, making it more difficult to reach the "ninety degree wrist angle at horizontal" position. The delay helps ensure a full, wide backswing, which in turn helps develop power and distance. Keep in mind, though, the longer, heavier club is also part of why the average golfer has trouble with his long irons and woods. They require more forearm and wrist strength to control—both before and after the forearm horizontal position—and maintaining the timing of the wrist and forearm action in the backswing and the downswing is more difficult.

Mulligan

Mark Your Scorecard Wisely

Scorecards have at least four, and sometimes as many as six, rows or columns in which to include scores for each member of the group. Rather than merely recording scores, though, carry a second scorecard to track your shotmaking.

I carry a second card on which I title the rows or columns with Score, First Shot, Second Shot, Third Shot, and Putts (e.g. S, 1, 2, 3, P). If I hit a good drive, I put a checkmark; if not, I put down the club I used. A good drive does not have to be in the middle of the fairway, only good enough to allow me to make the second shot the hole demands. A drive in the short rough gets a checkmark; a drive in a fairway bunker, in deep rough, or worse, does not. A par on a par three will have a scorecard marked with a three, a checkmark, two blanks, and a two for the number of putts. Repeat this for each shot on each hole and at the end of the day not only will you have your score, but you will also have a clear idea of which clubs and which types of shots were your challenge that day.

Repeating this over the course of a few weeks when you are playing regularly will be even more useful to your game. We all have days in which one club or another is working well, and others are not. Over the course of time, however, this kind of recordkeeping will clearly tell you the shots and the clubs that need work.

The Swing

Maintaining a Balanced Swing

Swing balance and leg movement are poorly understood parts of the game for the amateur golfer. They are also parts of the swing which receive the least amount of study and analysis.

Understandably so. They are complicated to explain and complicated to get correct. Although some problems can be counteracted by adjustments elsewhere in the swing, balance and leg movement problems are not in that category.

First, a few general points:

1) Focusing on the long clubs, your weight is initially about evenly distributed left to right. This means your center of gravity has to be at about the middle of your body—roughly in line with your navel.

    Swing Tip: The center of gravity should move to the back very little between address and the top of the backswing. If you ever feel like you are swaying, which can occur when trying to hit the ball hard, your center of gravity is likely moving too much.

2) In the backswing, the arms, shoulders, and back must rotate around the center of gravity. Doing so coils the upper body, providing the spring-like force needed to hit the ball hard.

3) Maximum power can only be developed if both parts of the swing are correct—the coiled rotation must be around the center of gravity, and the uncoiling must be accompanied by a slight forward shift of the location of the center of gravity.

So, how do you do all this? You can't easily think about, or focus on, your center of gravity and whether it is moving one way or the other. What you can do is focus on your back leg and knee. As you coil your upper body during the backswing, the back knee will stay flexed but at the same time the muscles in that leg will firm up and provide a foundation for the coiled power in your upper body. You should feel like your weight is moving slightly onto the inside of the back leg. But as you do so, you will also have the feeling your upper body is rotating and not shifting laterally. The combined sensation of increased weight on the back leg and rotation of the upper body means your center of gravity is not moving laterally either, not by much anyway. If you are supple enough to have a big turn, you can think about getting your forward shoulder straight above the inside of the back leg, about where your center of gravity will be, at the top of the backswing. Doing so means you have to be rotating your upper body—lateral motion of the upper body cannot occur and at the same time have the forward shoulder above your center of gravity.

The forward knee is also flexed, but in the backswing is more relaxed and not firm like the back knee. Instead it rotates and bends slightly backwards, until at the top of the backswing it points a few inches behind the ball.

In the downswing, the center of gravity shifts slightly forward as weight is transferred to the forward leg. The knee positions, and their actions, are reversed. The forward knee shifts forward and the muscles in the leg firm up— the entire leg becomes the foundation for the power to be unleashed in the swing. The back knee also rotates forward and ends, at the top of the follow-through, pointing down the fairway.

The perfectly balanced swings we see better golfers have are in good part the result of their mastery of the intimate relationship between swing balance and leg action. The foundation of a balanced backswing is the back leg. The center of gravity shifts back only a bit during the backswing, but in a more pronounced manner shifts forward during the downswing. The forward leg receives the shifted weight, and provides the foundation for the power to be imparted to the ball. Work on these swing keys and your shots will be longer and straighter.

Mulligan

Stand Up

In the chapter *The Rest of the Stance,* I wrote about positioning the knees, back, rear end, and shoulders to get a properly-oriented stance. Some golfers get those body parts correctly positioned, but only by bending their knees too much, by leaning their back and head forward too much, and sticking their rear end out so much they are almost crouching over.

OK, the sentence you just read may be over the top, but you get the idea. The correct golf stance requires we get all of those body parts in the correct position, but in doing so we must make sure we remain reasonably upright.

An upright stance ensures the upper body's position is not constraining the movement of the arms and shoulders; a constrained upper body reduces the arc of our swing and thus the distance we can get from our clubs. An upright stance also makes it much easier to maintain good balance during our swing. Think about golfers you know or have played with—more often than not those who have unbalanced positions in their finish start with poorly established body positions at address.

An upright stance is also important in the putting game. As the chapter *Putting* will explain, an upright putting stance is important to allow the desired pendulum movement of the arms and shoulders. As an example, I was playing with a friend a number of years ago who was having trouble with putting distance control. He had a partially crouched stance; I suggested he stand up a bit more, allowing his arms and shoulders to more easily do the work of swinging the club back and through contact. The ball literally began jumping off his putter.

Stand up when you swing the club; you will see the results from doing so.

The Swing

From Address to the Top of the Swing

We've talked about the components of the first one-third of the swing, let's put them together in sequence:

1) Forward press.

2) The takeaway starts with the clubhead moving along the backward extension of the target line. Keep the clubhead low to the ground during the start of the swing. The forward arm will feel like it is moving the clubhead more back than up.

3) The swing continues with the arms, along with the shoulder rotation, pulling the club upward. The forearms will begin to feel like they are moving more upwards than to the back.

> Swing Tip: A question frequently arises whether the shoulders should start rotating at the same time as, or after, the hands, wrists and arms start moving back. There is no "one size fits all" answer. Many writers say the shoulders should start moving a millisecond or two after the hands, wrists, and arms have started the backswing. I don't disagree.

4) Your weight will shift only slightly backwards, and your center of gravity will not move much from near its initial position. Do this by keeping a firm, tensed back leg and knee and moving your weight only slightly onto the inside of the back foot.

5) As your swing continues, your forward knee will flex back a bit, eventually pointing behind the ball.

Mid-backswing. Forward arm extension, back leg and side remain in position, forward knee points behind ball.

6) The wrists will cock at the point which is natural for your swing. For some, but not all, golfers, the wrist cock will be complete shortly after the forward forearm is parallel to the ground. From this point on, the arms raise and the shoulders rotate to get the club to the top.

7) The shoulder rotation continues around the neck (focus on the top of the spine as the specific point around which the shoulder rotates). The upper body does not shift laterally. Don't stop this rotation until the forward shoulder is under the chin, if you can turn that far, but do not go farther than is comfortable. The forward arm will have continued to be fully extended up and behind the head; the back arm and elbow

will be comfortably positioned—neither tight to nor extended away from the body.

8) Both the hips and shoulders rotate, but the hips rotate less than the shoulders, about half as much, and the hip rotation is completed before the shoulder rotation is complete.

9) The head may rotate slightly back, depending on how supple you are and despite the longstanding golf myth of a still head. However, your eyes never leave their focus point, which should be the point on the ball you want the club to make contact with.

Top of backswing.
Shoulders and hips have rotated, back leg has remains in position,
forward knee points behind ball.

10) At the top of the swing the body may be as much as halfway behind the ball, though, like the timing of the wrist cock, this also varies among better golfers.

I have not written about the front foot. Some golfers raise it up off the ground during the backswing, Jack Nicklaus and Tom Watson for example. Others don't, Nick Faldo and Greg Norman were in this category. I think amateur golfers are better off if they slightly raise the outer edge of the front foot, with the inside edge—from the big toe to the inside edge of the heel—on the ground. Doing so makes it easier to fully turn the hips and shoulders. But don't raise it by much, because to do so can work against the development of the coiled power in the hips and shoulders you want in your swing. It can also lead to poor front leg and shoulder action in the downswing, both of which can cause a loss of distance and poor directional control.

I have also not written about the club's position at the top of the backswing. The average golfer does not need to go past horizontal, or, for that matter, does not need to get to horizontal, but otherwise the point at which your swing stops is a personal comfort choice. If you can get to horizontal, keep control of the club, and get good distance, great. But if not, stopping short of horizontal should be the goal. The key in golf is not to get every possible extra yard of distance, but to control the swing so your distances and directions for each club are reliable. So if you start spraying the ball, stop short of horizontal and get your consistency back.

Mulligan

That Swing Plane Thing

I have referred to but not written in detail about the swing plane, and will not dedicate a complete chapter to the subject. This *Mulligan* will have to do.

I am not saying the swing plane is not important, but it should be thought of as a result of good things in the golf swing, not a cause of those good things. What do I mean? Simply stated, if a golfer does everything else this book says to do, the result will be an "on plane" golf swing.

To prove that statement, I went through my notebook of magazine clippings to study swing plane examples. I studied a series of articles in which professional golfers were pictured from the front, from behind the ball looking down the target line, and from down the target line looking back. These simultaneously-taken triplicate pictures are not as often published as they used to be, but are useful to study when they are available.

Looking at each golfer from behind, I found the angle of the forward forearm from vertical at the top of the backswing never varies outside the range of about 30° to 35°. The names of the golfers I looked at are all well-known—from Jack Nicklaus to Greg Norman to John Daly in the power hitter examples, Tom Watson, Steve Elkington, and Davis Love in the smooth swinging category, and Phil Mickelson and Tiger Woods in whatever category you want to put them. There were others as well, but you get the idea. Each of these great golfers have their own unique swing characteristics, but all ended up in the nearly the same position at the top. There must be something about this position important for hitting the ball.

But, you say, how can this help me? I cannot be stopping and trying to measure the forearm angle when I am playing, or even when I am on the range!

Fair question. In looking at the pictures, I realized their hands, at the top of the backswing, were typically slightly farther from the body than a point directly above the back shoulder. Their hands never came closer to the head than above the shoulder, and similarly never went farther from the head more than slightly away from a vertical line above the shoulder. A rather small amount of variation.

So, you now say, how can I use this information? First, work on everything else in this book and your swing plane should be fine. Then focus on the hands-to-shoulder position covered in the last paragraph. If you can get to the point where you think your hands are in the correct position—the position I described above—you are probably swinging "on plane." If you are not sure, find a pro whom you trust to help you determine whether you are or not.

Truth be told, I started looking into this when my teaching pro showed me a video of my swing plane—it was obviously too upright. I realized not long thereafter my high school golf coach had told me long ago to swing more around my shoulders, but never explained why. He had apparently noted my upright swing plane and was trying to correct it. Better if he had noted I had poor arm position in the backswing, and poor use of my arms in the start of the backswing, both of which I have worked on correcting to get the swing plane I want. Take this lesson with you next time you get to the range. If something is not right, make sure you know what is causing the problem, and fix it, not something else that may be the result of the problem.

The Swing

Starting Down

Now the fun part—hitting the ball. You're all cranked up, let's get to it.

You may have read the downswing is a reversal of the backswing, and that if you think from the reversal perspective you should be able to get the downswing started correctly. I don't agree. A lot of things have to happen to correctly get the club to the top, and a lot of things have to happen to correctly get the club going back down. They are not necessarily mirror image actions. For example, most amateurs know the lower body should start the move down, but lower body movement is not the last thing most do in the backswing. So work on your backswing, and work on your downswing. Don't confuse the two by a reversal thought process.

A first message about the downswing is that several actions must happen in a short timing sequence, and almost simultaneously. Whether you think one or the other is first is not terribly important.

I focus the start of the backswing on the lower body. If the front foot has been raised off the ground during the backswing, the downswing should start by replanting the foot on the ground, thus preparing the body for the weight shift occurring shortly thereafter. To do so, you need to move your forward knee and hips toward the target also, so these actions are essentially simultaneous. Whether you raise the forward foot or not, a good swing thought during practice sessions is to shift the hips forward enough to allow the forward foot to be fully planted on the ground. This move enables the forward side to firm up, from the foot through the knee to the hip. This firming action is important, as it will allow the forward side to act as a wall against which the body's power can be transmitted to the clubhead and the ball.

Hip movement forward at the start of the downswing.

Hip movement forward continues.
No change in wrist and arm relative positions.

Hips fully rotated at middle of downswing.
Wrists and forearms ready to uncock.

The movement of the lower body begins the club's downward move by forcing the hands and arms down in response to the movement of the lower body and hips. The club's move continues with the back arm and elbow tucking up against the body. You will often read about the tuck as if it is something you need to actively work to do. I believe the tuck should happen automatically as a result of the rotation of the shoulders that is initiated by the lower body shift forward—the forward shoulder rotating up, the back shoulder rotating down, both rotating around the top of the spine and beginning to reverse the backswing's rotation. The head stays still, and behind the ball.

The wrist-to-forearm angle has not changed, and the arms have not yet started to pull the club down. The movement of the clubhead has been the result of the movement of the lower body.

The swing continues with the forward hip beginning to rotate, further enabling the weight shift toward the target. The back knee moves laterally forward a bit, but it follows the hips and forward knee in a passive move, it does not actively work itself forward. The head remains still, behind the ball, and the spine angle established at address has not changed.

Your upper body, from the waist up, should stay behind the ball. A vertical plane perpendicular to and intersecting the target line at the ball should split your body about between the hips, or even perhaps a bit more forward. (Yes, I know that is a complicated sentence; I started out life as a mathematician and is how I think even now. Sorry.)

As the hip rotation and forward weight shift both near completion, the arms begin to really pull the clubhead down. This is the point in the downswing during which the clubhead speed needed to hit the ball hard begins to be developed. The arms begin to pull down hard and forcefully, still in tempo with the rest of the swing and not out of sync with the rhythm you developed earlier, and mostly with the forward hand (e.g. the upper hand on the club). The other hand's action is yet to come, and the wrist-to-forearm angle has only slightly changed. We'll talk about those subjects in the next chapter.

Mulligan

Watch the Best Swings of the Best Pros

The golf swing is hard for amateurs to master; we each have our own weaknesses. We are fortunate to have so much digital information available to be able to look at how the pros avoid the weaknesses that are our own golfing crosses to bear.

My challenge is swinging too much from my upper body. I do not take advantage of the powerful muscles in the lower body from which the pros obtain so much of their power and consistency.

Virtually all pro golfers have a strong move down that starts from the hips; one I like to study is Jack Nicklaus. Surprisingly, I do not mean the Nicklaus of the 1960s and early 1970s. Clips of Jack in those early years show a swing that was fast and of course powerful. Later in his career—particularly in clips of group demonstrations—you will see a slower swing. For that reason, it is easier to see his pronounced hip move forward at the beginning of the downswing. The hip move was a source of a large part of Jack's power. The failure to make the hip move Jack mastered is a reason we do not have the power we would like. It is a weakness of mine.

Your weakness may be rhythm and tempo. Tom Watson has a fast swing, but his rhythm has always been perfect. Take a look. Phil Mickelson is an acknowledged short game genius; there is no one better to watch if you are trying to improve your short game.

Take advantage of what the pros can teach you.

The Swing

Swinging Through the Ball

The average golfer concentrates less on swinging through the ball than he should. This part of the golf swing involves a shift from the actions of the body's large muscles—the arms, shoulders, legs, and hips, all of which are essential to getting the body ready for the clubhead's contact with the ball, to the actions of the small muscles—the wrists, forearms, and hands, which are the keys to the proper release of the clubhead. It is a golfing mistake not to fully understand and practice proper technique for swinging through the ball.

Let's first take a step back to make sure we understand the logic of what has to happen in this part of the swing. At address the clubhead is behind the ball pointing down the target line. All we have to do is get back to the same clubhead-to-ball-to-target-line orientation to hit the ball solidly and straight. It is simple to say. It is not simple to do.

What have we learned so far related to returning the clubhead to a target line orientation? First, start with a neutral grip, so as not to have a built-in tendency for slicing or hooking. Second, make sure the set-up, stance, and orientation at address have the club pointing straight down the intended target line. Third, at the start of the swing take the club back along an extension of the target line. Fourth, start down from the top with the correct sequence of actions to return to the orientation at address and allow the ball to be hit straight down the target line. All of these points together lead to an all-square position of the clubhead at ball contact. It is also called the neutral position or the neutral release position.

The all-square position simply means the face of the club points straight down the target line. This position results naturally from a swing path that has, immediately before and immediately after ball contact, a clubhead that is inside the target line. In other words, the swing path is inside to square to inside as the clubhead approaches, contacts, and moves past the ball's initial position. In a sense this might be considered the theoretically perfect swing path because it results from doing everything perfectly up to this point in the swing. It is fair to say it is perhaps the most difficult to attain on a regular basis.

Let's think about what might happen if our swing plane is from the inside, say by three degrees, and after ball contact continues on that plane, three degrees outside the target line. Two results are possible. First, if our clubhead is pointing outside the all-square position by exactly the same three degrees, we would expect the ball to go three degrees outside the target line. A dead push.

But what if the clubhead is pointed down the target line at impact, with a swing plane three degrees inside to outside? Without getting into all the physics of golf ball dynamics, the result is a counterclockwise spinning ball that hooks. This has been called the hook position at impact, the anti-slice position at impact, and quite a few unprintable phrases. A strong grip makes this ball contact position easier to develop. Experienced players often try to develop this swing path because balls with a hook spin tend to roll farther.

The opposite of the hook position at impact is the fade position, or anti-hook position. The fade facilitates consistency in both direction and distance with a ball tending to fly higher and land softly. The fade position has the clubhead pointing down the target line at ball impact, and is accompanied by an outside to inside swing path. The clubhead's movement from outside the target line before ball contact to inside the target line after contact results in a clockwise spinning ball that fades. The fade is frequently used by the best players to ensure swing and ball flight reliability under the pressure of competition.

To complete the set of ball contact positions, an outside to inside swing with a clubhead at the same angle from the target line as the swing path results in a pulled ball.

Now let's talk about what you need to do with the wrists, forearms, and hands to swing through the ball and have the ball contact position you have decided is best for your game.

First, though, consider another story I heard long ago. As the story goes, when Annika Sorenstam, who was a good athlete in a number of sports in her youth, decided to focus on golf, her father would not let her take a full swing until after weeks, if not months, of practicing her hand, wrist, and forearm action before, at, and after contact with the ball. The purpose was to ensure her timing at the moment of ball contact was smooth and consistent, and imparted maximum energy to the ball. If true, Annika's father should be given great credit for getting her swing on a developmental road leading to her incredible career.[2]

I am not sure this drill is taught any longer, but when I learned the game we were told to put our feet together and swing back only far enough to get the club parallel to the ground, then swing through and past ball contact until the follow-through had the club parallel to the ground. We were not to rotate our hips during this drill. You will find the only way to get solid contact with the ball is to have your hands, wrists, and forearms work together in unison at the moment of ball contact. When you get all those body parts working together, you will be amazed how far you can hit the ball.

Why is this drill useful? At the end of the last chapter I said the angle between the wrists and the forearms does not change in the part of the swing I called *Starting Down*. The release is the reason why. If the angle changes, it can only do so by releasing the clubhead early, thus breaking down the stored tension in the hands and wrists. Having stored tension, and a properly timed release of that stored tension during the downswing, is what gives good golfers the distance they get. It is what we all should be trying to develop in our swings.

So what does swinging through the ball mean? After the body starts the downswing, with the arms, shoulders, legs, and hips getting the club into position for ball contact, the "action" in the swing must move from the larger to the smaller muscles. The back shoulder must continue down and under the

---

[2] As with my Davis Love story in the Philosophizing chapter, I have not found a recent source to confirm this story. If not accurate, my apologies to Annika and her father.

Full extension at contact, body behind the ball.

Full extension toward target during follow-through.

head, with the forward shoulder moving up and out of the way. The forward weight shift must be appropriately timed. The back arm must be fully extended so both arms are fully engaged to ensure solid contact with the ball. These are actions of the large muscles in the swing, but happen before the actual release of the muscles important in swinging through the ball—those in the hands, wrists, and forearms.

At ball contact the wrists must fully uncock and, in fact, become cocked in the other direction. What does that mean? At the top of the backswing recall we said the back wrist was cupped and the forward wrist was straight, not cupped? The release means the back wrist fully uncocks and quickly moves into a forward position in-line with the forearm, or perhaps even past the in-line position, and the forward wrist becomes fully cocked. The back forearm and wrist briefly face forward of the body, turn over, and as the swing continues the back forearm ultimately points in a direction to the rear of the body. In my mind, this part of the swing is guided by, if not governed by, the back hand, though I am not sure everyone agrees with that view. Much of the power in the golf swing comes from the back hand; the release is how that power is unleashed.

The release does not mean the clubhead should immediately start to move inside the target line. The most consistent golf swings involve the movement of the hands and arms down and along the target line just after release, and not immediately moving to the inside. The movement inside occurs with the follow-through, which is what I write about in the next chapter.

Mulligan

Spend Time Practicing From the Mat

When wet or cold weather arrives many practice ranges require we hit from artificial mats. One range I frequent has so much play mats are used year around. Something to adjust to, but, sadly, adjust is something our golfing colleagues refuse to do. We have all heard the phrase "I hate hitting off these mats!"

The typical complaint is the clubhead's contact with the ball and the mat does not feel natural; the complaining golfer does not feel he can consistently take mat practice to the course. But *The Golf Channel* pros don't seem to have a problem, so why do so many amateurs?

The reason our friends complain about mats is they do not use their wrists and hands correctly before, at, or after contact with the ball. On turf they do not notice this weakness in their game because one way or another the clubhead ends up contacting the ball and the turf and perhaps making a divot as they complete their swings. If a golfer's wrist and hand action is not correct, the mat reacts responsively to the clubhead, and the reaction of the mat is felt in a different way than the clubhead feels from contact with the turf. Better golfers no doubt prefer turf as well, but they do not complain about mats because their wrist and hand action allows them to reliably contact the ball in a manner which minimizes, or perhaps even eliminates, the mat's responsive reaction.

Take the opportunity to work on the wrist and hand action in your swing. By swinging thru the ball correctly, with a properly timed release of the wrists and hands, you will soon forget any mental challenges you may have had about practicing on mats.

The Swing

The Finish

The thinnest section of my notebook of golf article clippings is titled *The Finish*. I don't know why. It may have been I never saw much about the finish that interested me, or I optimistically thought I had already mastered the finish. More likely, however, is that few articles focus on this topic because there is so much going on earlier in the golf swing thought to be more important.

It would be better if more articles, and more golfers, focused on the finish. As an example, let's start with a phrase long in use, but now only to remind golfers of something they should not have in their swing—the body position known as the "Reverse C."

If you can find an old picture or video of professional golfers prior to about 1980 you will find quite a few had swings with a Reverse C. One example is Johnny Miller. In his prime he was a tall and thin golfer; his swing reflected that build. He had a high finish, the club moving well above his shoulders as he completed his swing. His position at the finish usually included the classic perspective of the Reverse C.

The photo on the next page shows me, with a seven iron, in a Reverse C finish. My belt buckle points toward the target line. My shoulders are behind the belt buckle by several inches, with my left shoulder well behind my forward foot. The Reverse C shape formed by my back and right leg is evident, though perhaps not as dramatically as golfers from prior eras.

The Reverse C is not the ideal finish in the modern golf swing. It is a hard position in the long term for the back and spine. It is a hard position for the average golfer to attain and maintain good balance at the end of the swing. Finally, it is difficult to attain repeatability with, and good golf requires repeatability.

The Reverse C finish.
Although front leg is vertical, body from waist upward curls backward.

The modern, vertical stance, finish.

The finish of the modern golf swing is more around the shoulders than in the past. When looking at a modern golfer's finish, again from the perspective of across the target line, we see a straight vertical line from the forward foot up along the body through to the shoulders. The golfer's weight will be primarily on the forward foot, with the back foot only providing a balance point for the body's weight. All this adds up to the pose today's professionals have at the end of their swings.

How do we incorporate this modern finish into our golf swings? In a sense it is an automatic reflection of how well the earlier parts of the golf swing are carried out (which is another reason the golf magazines do not have articles on the finish for me to have clipped out over the years). At ball contact, in addition to our hands, wrists, and forearms performing the functions described in the *Swinging Through The Ball* chapter, the back shoulder should be moving down, under our head, and eventually forward and up to the finish position, all in a rotational move around our head and neck. The head should not move much behind the forward foot, a characteristic of the Reverse C. In conjunction with the rotational shoulder movement, the body's weight should end up primarily on the forward foot. The combination of these moves brings the head up to a more upright position than in the Reverse C. Combined with the release of the hands, wrist, and forearms through the ball and the full extension of the back arm down the target line at and after impact, the clubhead moves more around the shoulders. Done correctly, the back shoulder's rotation ends with it being up to, and perhaps slightly past, a vertical line with the forward knee. The better balance of this finish is a guaranteed reflection of everything that has come before.

We all have seen golfers who cannot get into this pose. Many do not extend their arms forward and down the target line, in particular their back arm, and end their swings with bent elbows and weight distributed between both feet. This is sometimes referred to as the "Chicken Wing," something we all want to avoid. Golfers who cannot get their weight forward will not be getting into the preferred vertical line finish and need to work on getting the body moving forward at and after contact.

The finish we all want is not hard to describe, and with work is not hard to incorporate into our games. It is worth the effort to do so.

Mulligan

Two Wrongs Don't Make a Right, Very Often

Think about the golf swings you see on television. Are they all exactly alike? No. Do they all work well? Yes. Some better than others of course, but they all work really, really well. If they are not all alike, what is the consistent theme we can extract from looking at these swings?

Let's take a frequently commented-on swing, specifically Jim Furyk's backswing. Not the standard swing we see on television, to be sure, but it has led him to win nearly twenty tournaments during his career. Not bad.

Furyk corrects his backswing's unusual characteristics during his downswing such that he is in perfect position at ball contact and during follow-through. So, essentially, his swing includes two nonstandard aspects allowing him to perform at the high level the PGA Tour requires. His swing is one in which two wrongs make a right.

There are other well-known professional golfers whose swings have also had wrongs—or perhaps I should say non-ideal aspects—incorporated in such a way to allow performance at high levels for a long time. Jack Nicklaus's flying right elbow was a subject of comment early in his career. Arnold Palmer's unusual follow-through needs no further description. Gary Player's follow-through had his balance shifting so much he often nearly, if not actually, made a step forward down the target line instead of being balanced on his forward foot.

These Hall of Fame golfers all made their swings work at never before seen levels of expertise and accomplishment. To the extent their swings had non-ideal aspects, they were all able to adapt or correct their swings to allow them to reach the top of their profession. It took a lot of practice, of course, but their success speaks for itself. What does this mean for us?

Take a good look at your golf swing, if you can get someone to video you, or, better yet, just sit down and think about how you swing? Do you feel like you are swinging more or less like they swing on TV? The answer is "no" for most of us. Do you feel like you only have one or two problems to correct? Again, the answer is likely to be "no."

Few amateurs get down to single digit handicaps, or are able to regularly hit the ball 250 or more yards. If you are happy with a handicap of 25 or so, these paragraphs can quickly be forgotten. But if you want to get down to, say, a 15 handicap, or lower yet, you need to think about what your problems are and start working on improving them. No one gets to be good at golf with significant swing defects. For the pros two or more wrongs might make a right and result in a zero handicap. For us, two wrongs make breaking 100 much harder. Set your goals for your golf game, list the improvements not just you want to make but also those you must make to get to those goals, and start working on your list the next time you are on the range.

The Swing

Tempo and Rhythm

Musicians know the difference between tempo and rhythm, but not all of us are musicians so let's make sure we understand these terms.

Tempo is speed. Military marches have fast tempos; ballads have slow tempos. Rhythm on the other hand is how the composer intends the tempo of the musical piece to be performed. Listen, for example, to *Take Five,* the great jazz piece by the Dave Brubeck Quartet. *Take Five* has a clear consistent tempo, but a unique, repeating rhythm. In golf we want to have an equally clear consistent tempo, but a smooth rhythm, not one that is erratic or inconsistent. The videos of Charles Barkley show an example of poor golf swing rhythm. We cannot have the unique rhythm in our golf games Dave Brubeck had in *Take Five* and be successful.

Arnold Palmer and Tom Watson were known to have fast tempos; Ricky Fowler also has a fast tempo. It is hard for the average golfer to have a fast tempo because doing so makes having a consistent and repeatable rhythm harder to attain. We are not Palmers, Watsons or Fowlers.

In the golf swing, consider rhythm to be the smoothness and repeatability of the movement. As the chapters you have just read say, we start our swing with the forearms, followed by the rotation of our shoulders, upper body, and hips. All of this while our weight is only slightly shifting back and the head is staying still. A golfer's ability to do all of these things smoothly with repeatability at the tempo he swings the club means he has good rhythm. We need to develop a good, repeatable rhythm and it is easier to do so if we do not have a fast tempo.

There are no simple rules to follow to develop good tempo and rhythm. There are no silver bullets in this part of the golf swing. Tom Watson has written of a golfer who used the song *Edelweiss* as a way to monitor his tempo. The first part of the word, "*Edel*" guided his swing up, the "*weiss*" part guided his swing down.

Ernie Els has written that a 1-2-3 count has helped him. The 1 is at the start back in the swing, the 2 is at the top, and the 3 is at contact. He has a smooth effortless swing; perhaps 1-2-3 is something to try.

A number of more recent articles have said the swing should follow a three to one ratio—the backswing taking three times as long as the downswing. Digital swing monitors sold today usually include a measurement of this ratio.

Sam Snead was still playing on tour when I learned the game; Sam had perfect tempo and rhythm. I still think about his swing when I am working on my tempo and rhythm. Find a pro to model your swing on and keep his, or her, swing's rhythm and tempo in mind as you practice.

Mulligan

Your Swing Thought

The nine chapters in *The Swing* section describe what is needed to have a good, reliable golf swing. I can imagine, however, you are now thinking "All well and good, but what am I supposed to think about when I try to put everything I have just read into practice?"

The next section, *On The Course*, will partially answer that question. Perhaps a more important answer than you will read in that section, however, is that you should think about any one of the things you just read about, or any one other thing I did not write about but which you have decided is important for your swing, but never more than just one thing.

Golf is too complicated to focus on everything I have written about all at once. With practice you will learn the keys to your swing—what to focus on to successfully carry out the shots the average round requires. When you learn what those keys are, pick the most important one and use it as your swing thought for your rounds.

You do not have to always use the same thought, but use one, and only one, for each round you play.

In my recent practice, I have found the sequence of motions occurring during the takeaway to be what I need to use as my swing thought. In fact, it is not the sequence of motions, but merely that I want my arms to start the swing along the backward extension of the target line before anything else moves. I won't change my swing thought until I feel like I have developed my takeaway into a reliable habit I do not have to think about any longer, in which case I will look for something else to focus on.

There are two caveats to my swing thought message. You may want a different swing thought for your putting stroke. OK. Putting is a different part of the game. Fair enough. Second, after you have played for a reasonable period of time, and are getting to know your swing's strengths and weaknesses, you may be able to occasionally add a second swing thought—provided it does not conflict with the first one. Here is an example of what I mean. The swing thought I have been using is obviously at the start of the backswing. Later in my swing, another weakness I have is a lack of reliability in the position of the hands and club at the top of the backswing. I have occasionally, after getting the backswing started, added a second swing thought at this later point in the swing—one focusing on getting the club in position at the top. I do this mostly on the range, but even on the range it means I have two swing thoughts.

After fifty-five years of swinging the golf club I feel like I handle an occasional second swing thought. But don't fool yourself into thinking what I am doing is easy. Until you fully understand your swing, it is best to focus on the one most important part of your swing that day and not overthink your game.

An Interlude:
Let's Talk about Slow Play

Slow Play. The real four letter words of golf.

Here are two examples of how golf course managers, and golfers, have not figured out the best way to address this problem.

Years ago, I was part of a group of golfers, three or four foursomes, playing a not overly difficult, but on this particular Saturday crowded, course. We were the first foursome in our group. Play had been steady, though certainly not quick. We were about two-thirds of the way through our round and came upon a relatively short par four, with groups on the green, in the fairway, and on the tee. There might have been two groups on the tee in front of us. We had to wait quite some time to hit our tee shots. When we did, the groups we were waiting on played rather quickly and as we arrived in the fairway to play our second shots the green was already open. A marshal came up as we were hitting and went into a detailed lecture on why we needed to play more quickly. An explanation of the facts of the situation was to no avail to the marshal, nor was it to the manager at the clubhouse after we finished our round. We elected not to return to the course in the future, and have not done so.

Similarly, at a different Houston-area course a few years later, I was part of a group waiting on the tee of a par three hole located near the clubhouse. We had a lengthy wait for the group in front to complete play. When we did tee off, two of our group hit their shots into the water in front of the green, which of course delayed our arrival at the green. The result was a similar conversation with both the marshal and the clubhouse manager, and we thus obtained a second course we do not play any longer.

What is the message in these stories? The message is not that the course marshals and clubhouse managers were out of line trying to maintain steady play. The message simply stated is circumstances will arise from time-to-time which appear to be but are not the result of slow play, and the usual warning to the apparently-at-fault group is not always the right answer.

Instead, golfers, course marshals, and clubhouse managers should focus on little things helping to keep the pace of play up to what it should be when all is well—when they are not waiting on the group in front of them and when balls are not errantly going into the water or the woods. If the pace of play during the "good times" of a round is on target, the time for the full round should be on target as well.

And those little things really are little. Be assured, I would not be writing this chapter if I had not seen everything I write about, and more, occur much too often.

----

1) Let's start at the tee. Not a common place for slow play problems to arise, but not unheard of either. Most of us walk to par four and par five tees with a driver or other wood club in our hand. As we should. But on par threes, when club selection may not be easy to determine, players will often stand and watch the tee shots of others before going back to the cart, make a final club selection decision, and return to tee off. Not taking a lot of extra time, to be sure, but in the vast majority of tee shots the choice will be between two clubs—why not pull them both out and not take the time to go back and forth?

2) If a group has players teeing off from different tees, for example the blue and the white, delays can occur in the transition from one to the other. The same messages apply. Players teeing from the shorter tee should have their clubs in hand while the other players are teeing off. They can then walk to their tee, or be ready to get in and out of the cart when they get to their tee. None of this prevents the golfer from maintaining the etiquette of watching the other player's tee shots. Groups should also consider letting the players using the shorter tees hit their balls first, if their drives are unlikely to reach the group in front.

3) What to do when the course has a "cart paths only" rule in place for a hole or for the entire course? (In the latter case the first option we should all consider is to walk!) Club selection is always harder when one cannot drive to the ball. But it is a rare cart path not having a few yardage markers on it, or nearby sprinkler heads with distances

marked. In the digital age we also have distance measurement tools in our carts and bags. Even if you cannot drive out to the ball, it is rarely difficult to get an accurate estimate of the length of your next shot. Take two or three clubs on the walk out—one will certainly be the club you need. (This is a real irritant to me—it is always the slowest walker who wants to go out, get an exact distance, go back to get the club, then go out again to hit the ball. Wake up people—if you want to take a walk go to a park!)

4) It is easier to maintain a good pace of play when carts are allowed in the fairway. But even on those days there are thoughts to keep in mind. If you are not the first player to play, the above messages about estimating distances, picking a club, and planning the shot can all be done while watching the shots of the other players. If you are the second player in your cart to play, get back in the cart after hitting the ball; put your club back in the bag when the cart stops wherever the next shot is to be played from.

5) If your game may occasionally require a provisional ball, keep a second ball in your pocket. On the tee this is not an issue, unless you are the last to tee off, because the rule book says provisional shots are struck after all tee shots have been completed. In the fairway or rough, if a provisional ball is needed, how hard is it to have a spare close at hand?

6) If someone in your group does need to hit a provisional ball, the rules provide for five minutes to look for the original ball (which, by the way, under the soon-to-be-approved new rules drops down to three minutes). The best way to keep pace of play up is for the other golfers to hit their next shot, then help look for the potentially lost ball. In most cases, if it is to be found, it will be found while the others are hitting their next shot, resulting in no lost time for the overall pace of play of the group.

7) Amateur golfers do not have tournament referees with the power to put them "on the clock," as tour pros do, so we need to be more aware of our surroundings to maintain the correct pace of play. If you get to a tee and the green in front of you is clear, check your pace of play.

Unless the course is not busy that day, it probably means you are slow. On the other hand, you may be getting pushed by the group coming up behind. If so, the message almost invariably is you are slow that day. In either of these cases make sure your group thinks about why it is slow and does something to correct it. More times than I like to remember I have been the one to say to the rest of my group "OK, guys, we need to pick it up." Not something any of us want to have to say; help your foursome out—think about whether you are the slow player, why you might be slow, and do something to correct it.

8) There are few Lee Trevino's in the golf world who can plan their shot, select their club, and hit the ball while carrying out a nonstop conversation with whoever may be nearby. (Although I have a friend who comes close!) Most amateurs (and pros for that matter) need, or at least prefer, silence to plan the shot, get the grip and stance set, and carry out the shot, and thus need to do things to not inordinately delay the rest of the group. Look down the fairway to plan your shot while others are doing so, or, while driving from the tee to the location of your ball, think about what will be necessary for the next shot to be successful. Is it the second shot on a par five? Do you want to hit it as far as you can, or is the goal to get a certain distance from the green in preparation for the third shot? If it is an approach shot, look for the pin position—independent of the distance from your ball to the green. If the pin is near the front, would you rather be slightly short of the green if you do not get the result you want, or have a longer putt from farther back on the green towards the pin? Is there a trap, a grass bunker, or water on any side of or short of the green? If so, what distance do you want to hit the ball to make sure the result is what you want, whether hit perfectly, nearly perfectly, or only marginally acceptably?

9) The green should be the easiest place to maintain a good pace of play, but as the song goes "It ain't necessarily so." There is no reason to carefully watch other player's strokes—after all there is no risk of a lost ball. You will want to do so for a variety of reasons of course—comradery, learning the speed and slope of the green—but while doing so you can be looking over your putt, perhaps walk around the green

to get an idea of the break and grain the ball will be subject to, and even begin to think about the stroke you need to make. All of this can be done while others are preparing for and making their putts.

10) Amateur golfers often do not realize the line of a putt may look completely different from behind the ball than it does from behind the pin. If you do not walk around the ball and pin, you may never appreciate those subtleties. I have a habit of circling the green as I walk up to repair my ball mark. Not only do I learn from what I see, but I can also sense in my feet the extent to which the green slopes one way or another. At my home course, which is a tough course with tough greens, it is essential golfers look at putts from all directions. Doing so as part of a routine as you first approach your ball is an easy and efficient way to do so. It can all be done while others are preparing for and putting, so the time required to putt your own ball will be short.

11) If you watch much TV golf you will have heard Johnny Miller complain when a pro stops, before putting his short last putt, to mark, re-clean, and replace his ball, with the line on the ball pointing exactly where he wants it. His point is just to get on with it and putt out. I agree. I have also heard it said that Jack Nicklaus does not think amateurs should mark their balls at all, unless obviously dirty or in the line of another golfer's putt. He makes a good point—what good does it do in a typical round to mark our balls?

12) There are other ways to speed up your play around the green. I know golfers who routinely park their golf carts five to fifteen yards short of the green, regardless of where their ball is, and walk to the green from there. After holing out, they have to walk back to their carts, in full sight of the players waiting in the fairway, where they take the time to mark their scorecards, after cleaning and returning their clubs to their bags, then driving to the next hole.

What sense does that make? Why not drive to the back of the green, park there, finish the hole, get back into the cart after the short walk from the pin to the cart, and drive to the tee where the clubs can be cleaned and the scorecard can be marked—while the group member teeing off first can be planning and carrying out his tee shot. So much faster, so much less irritating to the group behind, so much more in the manner intended for the gentlemanly game.

13) This applies to the 18th green as well. How many times have you watched a group hole out on 18, shake hands, walk to their carts, finish up with their score cards, and perhaps even clean and put away their clubs, balls and tees, before driving on?

How to tell if you are a slow player? It should be obvious, except when it isn't. If you are lucky, a friend or work colleague will say something, as happened to me many years ago. The friendly advice led to me always to be conscious of my pace of play, to the point where if I am in a slow playing group I tend to play too fast, in a usually unsuccessful attempt to get the group moving faster. Doing so does not generally lead to a better score.

Recognizing you are a slow player is not hard. Are you frequently part of a group letting other groups play through? Do groups behind you skip a hole to get ahead rather than wait to play each hole? Do others in your group drive down the fairway well ahead of you, either immediately after, or while you are preparing to hit, your shot? Do your golfing friends a favor and think about your pace of play.

Not all complaints about pace of play are appropriate. If you are behind a group playing at the recommended pace for the course, they are not playing slow. Deal with it—adjust your pace of play. If there is a group ahead of that group, they should not necessarily have to, or may not be able to, let you through. Enjoy the beautiful surroundings most courses offer. If you are a single or in a twosome, you will be faster than the group ahead of you. Deal with it.

A friend of mine and I took an afternoon off a couple of years ago and played a round at my home course. There were only a few groups on the course and we played good rounds at a steady pace. When we got done I happened on our club pro, who was listening to a golfer, who had played as a single and had come up behind us near the end of our round, complain about something. I realized later his complaint was about our pace of play and had a conversation with our pro the next day. It turned out such complaints were typical for the individual and no one ever saw him playing with anyone else, did they? He always played as a single, for good reason apparently.

My friend and I both had good rounds that day, and finished in under three hours. Complaints about slow play are appropriate—but only when they are appropriate.

This book provides ideas on what is necessary to develop a reliable, low scoring golf game. An implicit message of the words in this book is that good golf is a matter of developing automatically repeatable golf swing, and golf shotmaking, habits. Good golfers know that no real thought should be required for any given shot except the direction to and strength with which the shot must be made. All else must become second nature. If it does not, you risk consciously going through the same sequence of preparations I have written about in the chapters of this book, which can only lead to slow play. Avoid the slow play risk by working on your game on the range, preparing each shot as if it were on the course during a round, and getting to the point where detailed shotmaking thought is not required.

There is nothing worse than being behind a slow playing group, except perhaps being part of one. Keep these thoughts in mind and keep your pace of play up.

Mulligan

Times Change, or Do They?

We have all heard the phrase "Times Change." We have all also heard phrases saying, essentially, "If we wait long enough what goes around comes around." Both apply to the golf game, and the golf swing.

Ball position is a good example. As the *Ball Position* chapter explained, the guidance golfers are given has changed over the years. Anyone who regularly reads the golf magazines knows of golf fads that have come and gone. A few years ago the "Stack and Tilt" swing was all the rage, and a few touring pros adopted the technique. It has not been in the news in quite some time, though. No doubt the magazines have a different fad this year.

We might get back to the day when what I was taught in the early sixties about ball position comes back and is taught once again. Perhaps not. The key message from all this though is there are things a golfer must do to have a good, solid, reliable golf game, and there are things the golfer can adjust to his own liking.

This book does not distinguish between those two categories. A serious golfer has to decide some things on his own.

On The Course

Getting off the First Tee

The hardest shot for many golfers is on the first tee. Period, end of story.

It may be there are new members of the foursome, and we all want to do our best in front of new friends. It may be a group from the office, and, similarly, we all want to do our best with those with whom we work. It may be there is a long line of golfers waiting for their tee times and it is hard to do well in front of an audience. It could in truth be anything, but the first tee is the hardest shot for many of us.

On one hand, the tee shot, like all other shots, is merely the result of everything I have written about in this book. But combining all those words into a successful swing on the first tee is easier said than done. So, what should a golfer be doing and thinking about to get every round started off on the path we all want—a good solid drive in the fairway of the first hole?

The first thing to do, and not many golfers do in my experience, is start the day at the practice range. Do not hit an entire bucket, unless you spend a lot of time on the range every week and can easily do so before a round. Start by loosening up and getting the golf muscles remembering how to work together. Ideally, you have stretched before leaving for the course. The first club in your hand should be a short iron or wedge. Quarter, then half, then full swings. Get your tempo and rhythm back in your subconscious mind with these easy-to-swing clubs.

Next get a mid-iron, one you like to practice with. For a long time my club of choice was the five iron, but more recently have been picking up the six or seven. No reason, just felt like changing the routine. In warmup sessions I hit this club off a tee most of the time, and rarely off the ground. The idea is to get your body in a golf mode; intense practice off the ground is for a range practice session.

Finally, a driver or three wood off the tee, likely the first shot in your round. I only hit a few of these to get ready for the round—either you can hit this club well or you cannot. The warmup balls before a round will not significantly change anything.

Throughout your entire warmup routine, be thinking about your swing thought for the day, unless of course you have one in mind from your range work. If you are struggling with your game, for whatever the reason, you may need a different swing thought from week to week. But have one in mind for each round.

Over the years I have frequently focused on the movement of my back leg during the backswing as my swing thought. I have long had a tendency to sway back during the backswing. By focusing on keeping my back leg in the correct position, with my weight shift as I want it to be during the backswing, I avoid swaying and my on-course swings are more reliable.

A swing thought may not be what the touring pros are looking for. I have seen articles over the years in which the writer says, in essence, when you get to the tee, or address the ball from anywhere in the fairway, you should only be thinking about where you want the ball to go. But touring pros have a different game than we do, in all of the ways that are obvious and don't need to be enumerated.

I have also read of touring pros who like to hit their driver as the last part of their warmup, then go straight to the first tee as close to their tee time as they can. They keep the rhythm they have found on the range flowing into their round. We cannot always go straight to the tee and start our rounds immediately, so forget those first tee jitters. Go to the first tee with your swing thought in mind and hit the first ball like you have been on the range.

Mulligan

Concentrate

Years ago, when I was in graduate school, I could sit down at my desk and not get up for hours. Concentration was easy. You shut the rest of the world out and did what you had to do.

If only concentration were easy for our entire lives. Many things change with age; personal, family, and business pressures all make it harder to concentrate on one thing for long. Shutting out the rest of the world is not as easy, if doable at all, as it once might have been.

I've just come back from a practice round, one in which I was playing alone without the distraction of groups either in front or back. It should have been a situation in which I could concentrate on the part of my game I am working on without a problem. It worked for a few holes, then other things started to creep in and interrupt my concentration. I quit early.

Find something to focus on that allows you to block out the rest of the world when preparing for and taking each shot. Your game will be the better for it.

On The Course

Fairway Woods and Hybrids

Today's golfers are lucky—technology provides advantages past generations did not have. The technology in fairway woods and hybrids is a perfect example. These clubs are much easier to hit than the two and three irons some of us remember using—or trying to use—in past eras.

The swing for these clubs is not any different, in most regards, from the description in the section *The Swing*. The ball should be back from the forward heel, typically two to three ball's widths. The key is to ensure the bottom of the swing coincides with the location of the ball in the stance, so ball position is critical.

Here is a bottom of the swing test to use at the range. Place seven or eight balls in a line on the opposite side of the target line, each touching the next in the line. You will not have a ball or a tee in front of you, just the bare ground. Set your stance with the forward-most ball on a line extending away from your forward heel, perpendicular to the target line. Swing a fairway wood and a hybrid several times each. The place where your swing consistently contacts the ground is the bottom of your swing for these long clubs. Looking at the line of balls will tell you how far back in your stance the ball should be placed.

You may be wondering "What about your words in the *Ball Position* chapter?" If you go back and reread that chapter, you will see I did not give absolute positions, but said there was some personal preference involved. The bottom of the swing test will help you find your best ball position. For most golfers it will not be far from what I described in the earlier chapter.

I used to choke up on these clubs, but no longer do unless the ball is above my feet. I find it best to grip the club near the top, as with any other club for which I intend to make a full swing.

These clubs require the full arc of the swing, from setup to the top, down to ball contact, and continuing through to a balanced stance at the finish. Those are all the same swing characteristics described in earlier chapters, but they bear repeating here because so many golfers think hitting the ball off the ground with these clubs requires a different swing—perhaps shorter back, perhaps shorter finish, perhaps less of a weight shift, perhaps something else. They do not. Use your full swing and let the club do the work.

Some writers say to sweep the ball off the ground with these clubs; others say no, you must hit down on the ball. Those differing recommendations are in part semantics, but we need to understand how these clubs work to ensure we know how to use them correctly. For the driver on the tee, the ball is swept into the air with the force imparted by the clubhead. The club-to-ball contact point is, logically, just after the bottom of the arc of the swing. The driver gives the longest distance because it is the lowest loft club in the bag—a sweeping action with any higher loft would put the ball too high into the air.

Fairway woods and hybrids have more loft than drivers. A three wood is typically between 14.5° and 15.5°, and a three hybrid about 19°. Those higher lofts mean the ball should not be struck after the bottom of the swing, but rather at, or perhaps just before, the bottom. The contact of the club with the ball is, therefore, not a sweep in the sense used for the driver, but instead is a hard driven smash, with the loft giving the ball the intended flight path and distance. Because these clubs are frequently used from the fairway, or rough where the lie may not be perfect, the "hard driven smash" thought is a good one to have in mind to ensure solid contact.

Adjustments are required to successfully use these clubs from the rough. Ball position should be farther back so a minimum amount of grass is trapped between the face of the club and the ball. The swing may need to be more upright, to further minimize the effect of the grass behind the ball. But do not overdo this—if the ball is sitting too far down the likelihood of a positive outcome is low enough that a better decision may be to use a seven iron, followed by a wedge to the green for a one putt par.

Mulligan

Get a Round in on the Range

Going to the range to practice is not always fun, but needs to be done to get better looking scorecards. A way to make the time go by with a valuable outcome is to play a round on the range.

After warming up, hit the shot you would need to hit on the first tee of your home course. Then honestly gauge how well you hit the ball, and decide what the second shot would be on the hole. Continue on to the green, then move to the second tee and continue the process throughout your home eighteen holes.

This routine has several advantages. You get a round's worth of swings in, without the time required to move through the course. Your body gets a good variety of practice in. Your mind gets the routine of thinking what you need to do on your home course. Finally, you learn what shots to practice the next time you are on the range for a session of woodshedding your swing.

Long Irons

Before hybrids were invented, golf instruction books spoke of long irons (1-3), mid-irons (4-6), and short irons (7-9). In recent years, as the traditional long irons have been removed from many amateur's bags, the "new long irons" are the four iron, for the few still carrying it, and the five and six irons. One might think we have eliminated the hardest clubs in our bags to hit, and we have, but we have also replaced those clubs with several others.

Think about it. We play the woods and hybrids fairly often, and the second group of clubs getting a good workout in a typical round include the seven, eight and nine irons, and perhaps also the six iron. The four or five irons? They have become our hardest clubs to use. But how many of us spend a lot of time on the range practicing those clubs? Not many in my experience, and I include myself in that group.

The challenge is these are our lowest lofted irons, but we cannot swing them like we do the higher lofted irons. The low lofts makes solid contact harder, especially given the longer shafts. Those two facts—low lofts and longish shafts—lead the average golfer to have too much tension in the body and the brain, which is the wrong thing to do with these clubs.

I find that long irons, more than other clubs, require a focus on relaxation from shot preparation to address to swing. Repeat the ball position exercise described in the *Fairway Woods and Hybrids* chapter for these clubs. The correct ball position for most golfers will be three to four balls inside the forward toe, farther back than for woods and hybrids.

The combination of small club faces and long-ish shots means the importance of certain aspects of the swing must be overemphasized, or perhaps better said "must be over-focused on," during practice. Weight distribution should be biased forward. I tend to point my knees inward even more, to help ensure proper weight distribution.

The forward shoulder should be higher than the back shoulder, with more emphasis on this point than for other clubs. Because these are our hardest clubs to hit, every aspect of the full swing needs to be focused on with particularity. The clubhead should start smoothly back with a uniform motion of the club, hands, and arms, the hips only moving after the upper half of the body is well into the swing. The clubhead needs to be taken straight back in a full, long arc, ensuring maximum power is imparted to the ball.

I need to ensure I swing at my desired tempo and rhythm, and as a result my driving range practice with these clubs focuses largely on that point.

The weight shift forward and rotation of the hips out of the way of the body on the downswing are both particularly important (these clubs have a lot of particularly important aspects for successful shots). This is a result of the fact the ball is not swept off the ground, but rather is struck before the bottom of the arc of the swing. That contact point maximizes the power with which the clubhead hits the ball and allows the club's loft to initiate the ball's flight on the intended path. These are hard, solid, full power swings. (Think hard driven smash here also.) With practice they can in fact be both more fun and easier to carry out than other shots. There is nothing better than to watch a ball, having been well hit with a four or five iron, fly along its intended flightpath.

As the swing moves down to and past the ball, concentrate on getting the back shoulder down and under the chin, and follow-through to the end of the swing.

It is best to practice these clubs on tees first. I tee the ball only slightly higher than if it were sitting on the grass—from a distance the difference would not likely be visible.

On the course, long irons should rarely, if ever, be used if the ball is sitting down in the rough or for significantly downhill lies. The better part of valor is to use a higher lofted club followed by a pitch or chip to the hole for a one putt par.

Mulligan

Forget the Divot

We have all seen it. The shots by tournament players on television ending with a large divot flying down the fairway for the caddie to retrieve. And we all wonder "How can I learn to do that?"

I used to wonder the same thing, until I heard or read that not all the best players take a large divot, and often don't take much of a divot at all. For some clubs, iron shots for example, it is a fact the club will usually contact the ground. But a big divot is not essential for good golf. There are other things in the golf game to worry about, but the size of the divot should not be even near the top of your list.

So forget about the divot. Completely. Just forget about it.

On The Course

Short Irons

Let's get one thing clear about these clubs. The goal is not to hit the ball as far as you can; the goal is to be accurate in distance and direction. Repeat. The goal with your seven, eight, and nine irons, and your wedges, is to be accurate in distance and direction.

Yes, we have all seen the touring pro on television who hits his eight iron 180 yards, or more. But they are touring pros. Their golf games are different than ours. Their clubs are different than ours. Let them do it. We should be figuring out what distance we can reliably hit an eight iron.

There is not much to say about using these clubs. They do not require a hard swing. The ball will be at or back of the middle of the stance, which will be narrower than for your longer clubs. Your backswing may not always go all the way back.

To "not swing hard" does not mean you do not need good clubhead speed. These clubs may involve taking a divot and good clubhead speed is required to keep the club moving at and through impact with the ball and ground. For that reason, wrist and forearm action just before and at impact is essential.

Your weight will be biased forward with these clubs, say sixty percent or so, perhaps more, and certainly more with your wedges. As is generally true, your weight should be biased to the inside of each foot; I ensure this by pointing my knees inward during my setup. The forward shoulder will be higher than the back. This combination of weight distribution and shoulder position may seem at odds with each other, but they work together to maximize the likelihood of the clubhead's solid contact with the ball.

Your backswing will not go quite as far back along an extension of the target line as it does for longer clubs. I sometimes feel like I take the club inside a bit earlier, doing so with a nearly full turn back as the arms and shoulders complete the backswing. My sense is this gets me into a position allowing a smooth weight shift and start of the backswing, and gives reliable short iron performance.

Note I am not summarizing the swing that results in a ball hitting the green, taking two bounces, and backing up toward the fairway by eight or ten feet. Though frequently seen on television, those shots are beyond the scope of this chapter, and this book.

To be successful with these clubs, you need to complete a full turn of the body down and through contact, accompanied by the forward weight shift, with the hands finishing high. I have written this message in other chapters, but once again I find rhythm and tempo to be very important with these clubs.

Everything you have just read about using these clubs could easily be accompanied by the phrase "in most instances." In most instances means good lies in the fairway, or if in the rough a ball that is sitting up reasonably well. Balls in the fairway but with bad lies, say old unfilled divot holes, or in the rough and sitting down, need to be farther back in the stance. Your shoulder position may need to be adjusted for the slope of the ground, and your weight will likely need to be more forward. Don't forget to check your club selection because most of us cannot get our usual distances from difficult lies.

These should be shots you do not have to overthink. You should know which club to use immediately after determining the distance to the pin. Because these should be clubs you spend a lot of time with on the range, the outcome should be predictably good.

Mulligan

The Short Game

My message in the *Mulligan* titled *Two Wrongs Don't Make a Right, Very Often* was, in essence, we cannot have too many unusual aspects of our golf swings if we are to have a reliable, successful golf game. We need to focus on getting the basics of the game, from the grip to the follow-through, as close as we can to what the experts have found to be best.

The short game is different. There are aspects of the short game we need to learn using the techniques the experts say we should use. But there are also aspects we can, and should, use our own sixth sense on. The short game has many shot dependent considerations—overall distance, distance to the edge of the green, distance from the edge of the green to the pin, lie, turf… You get the idea. All this means fixed rules which can be written to apply to the rest of the game cannot necessarily be written for all situations in the short game.

The following four chapters will cover the rules that can be written. But Phil Mickelson did not get his short game genius reputation by following the rules everyone else followed. He got it by looking at each situation he faced and by coming up with the shot necessary at the time.

We may not get to the level where Phil has been so often for so long, but it is not a bad goal to have in our minds when we are faced with something we have not faced before.

The Short Game

Pitching

First, let's define what we mean by "pitching" the golf ball. Say you are standing in front of a green trying to decide what shot to hit. If you were to throw a ball, what would be the natural way to get the ball to end up near the pin? (The throw has to be underhanded). Would your natural throw be relatively high in the air, trying to have the ball land softly and stop relatively quickly? If the answer is yes, you know what a pitch shot is.

The pitch shot should be one of the easiest, most reliable shots in your golf game. For me, the sixty yard pitch is one I feel like I can do just about any time. I usually use a 54° sand wedge but, depending on how I feel about the shot, including how hard or soft the turf is, I may switch to my 58° lob wedge or perhaps even to my 50° gap wedge. This is not a shot to try to hit hard, so use the club that you are most comfortable with, in other words that works best for you without conscious thought. That distance may not be sixty yards, either, but should be somewhere between roughly forty and eighty yards. The key is to find the club and the distance you are comfortable with, and practice to understand how your swing works for that club and distance. Then expand out to other distances.

My feet are closer together than shoulder width. I generally use a square to the target line stance—a line across the front of the toes will be parallel to the target line—but many golfers drop the forward foot back away from the target line. Take care, though, as I find that opening my stance for pitch shots leads me to pull the ball more than intended. I find it just too easy to let the lower hand take over and not allow the follow-through to continue down the target line.

Weight distribution should be about 70% on the forward foot, a comfort thing more than an exact 70%.

Front to rear weight distribution should be balanced between the balls and the heels of the feet; I bend my knees a bit more than for longer shots. A line dropping straight down from the front of my knees is likely a bit behind the balls of my feet. Some golfers nearly have their shoulders over the balls of the feet, particularly for shorter pitch shots.

If your weight is correctly balanced, your body will feel more comfortable than perhaps for any other swing.

The ball will generally be no farther forward than midway between the center of the stance and the back heel, and often—with practice you will learn when—even farther back.

Why, you say, do we see the professionals on television with the ball farther back? One reason is they are professionals and are trying to do more things with the ball than we amateurs can or should try doing. Most of the time they are trying to hit the kind of shot I said in the last chapter was beyond the scope of this book—one that hits short of or at the pin, takes two or three bounces forward before stopping or pulling back. We are just trying to master the simple, straightforward pitch shot that ends up at the distance we want. Remember that long ago professionals started out as we do. When we have mastered the shot described in this chapter, we can try to develop the shots they use routinely.

The swing for this shot is smooth and rhythmic, and not a full swing. With your feet this close together, using a full swing risks loss of balance.

You may be asking "So, what do I do inside of forty yards, in the yardage gap shorter than you have just described, but longer than is covered by the *Chipping* chapter?" A fair question. It is a somewhat different shot in a number of ways.

The stance and ball position are different. Most golfers pull the forward foot back from the target line several inches, perhaps as much as five inches (this is a comfort-dependent decision), and pointed more forward toward the target. The ball will be farther back, perhaps even in line with the back heel, with that toe pointed behind the ball. Some better golfers use ball positions even farther back, to increase control of the ball's flight and amount of roll.

Body weight will still be biased forward, and balanced between the balls of the feet and the heels. The posture at address should be comfortable and not hunched over.

Your swing should be smooth and largely in the shoulders and arms. I have two main swings for this type of shot: a full swing in which the clubhead gets above shoulder height, and a half swing in which the shaft of the club gets slightly above parallel to the ground.

The key to the pitch shot for any distance is that the action of the forearms and wrists has to be firm and smooth throughout the swing. The backswing must have wrists that are cocked midway back, and a firm, equally smooth downswing in which the back hand in particular guides the wrist uncocking and firm contact with the ball. The follow-through should be along the target line until the club gets about parallel to the ground, at which point the movement of the body onto the forward leg may result in a swing more around the forward shoulder than it is for longer shots.

You have probably heard a golfer say "I quit on that one." What that golfer meant is he lost the firm action in his hands and wrists—he did not timely uncock his wrists, and/or he did not continue his arm action through contact with the ball. As a result, the clubhead did not solidly contact the ball and insufficient forward momentum was provided to successfully have the ball land at the target distance.

Wrist and arm action are key to this shot—to ensure the correct ball flight, the correct final distance, and the correct amount of roll (which should not be much) after the ball hits the ground.

Mulligan

Take Notes Along the Way

I have a folder on my desk with eight pieces of paper in it, ranging in size from about three inches by four inches (obviously torn out of a small notebook long ago) to six inches by nine inches. One of the pieces is an old scorecard I must have found in a cart because none of the names on the card are mine. Other than one I wrote in the last few weeks, I have no idea how old these pieces of paper are. I also have a handful of small notebooks in my golf bag and in various drawers or boxes, each also of an indeterminate age.

The one consistent fact is they all have notes I have taken on the practice range or, sometimes, after an actual round. Each of these notes has the same theme—they document something I thought at the time worked for my game, or I needed to work on, or I wanted to try on the range, or might even have been something I wanted to make sure I did not do again. Here is an example of what one says:

"54° Wedge

    Lt. foot just a bit back from line of play

    Ball inside right foot a bit

    Watch posture, do not slump

    Focus on ball thru contact

    Slow back, smooth wrist cock/uncock

    Right foot can turn out a bit."

There is more but you get the idea—this piece of paper includes a rather detailed analysis of what I thought I learned that day while practicing my 54° wedge. The notes continue with the distances the ball will go when the club goes back to nearly parallel to ground and when it goes 35° to 45° past parallel.

I am not sure I still follow exactly what these notes say, but I would not have written them down if they did not seem to work. The notes gave me something to develop further in the future, or, if I get haywire with this club, they give me something to go back to when trying to correct my problems.

If you are serious about golf, you will keep a small notebook in your golf bag and take notes along the way.

The Short Game

Chipping

If the high, soft pitch shot I described in the last chapter does not feel right, a low running chip shot is the answer. There are a lot of reasons to prefer this shot—the turf may not be to your liking for a wedge, you may be near the green and the pitch shot will not feel right (and in fact will not be right), or perhaps it is a windy day and you do not want to get the ball high in the air.

This is a shot to be adapted to personal preferences—there are only a few, rigidly applied, chipping rules. The par three course I grew up on had a long wide practice green, and I remember hours of chipping practice on that green. I have no idea if my stance was what is now recommended, if my weight distribution was what is now recommended, or if my swing was what is now recommended. The hours of practice gave me a pretty reliable chipping game though, which is what we all want.

The stance in particular is an example of how this shot can be adapted to personal preferences. Some golfers narrow their stance slightly, pulling their forward foot back from the target line and turned toward the target a fair amount. Those golfers may also turn their back foot back. I have seen golfers that maintain a relatively standard stance with the only change from the full shot with a given club being that the feet may be slightly closer together. I have also seen golfers with their feet very close together, the forward foot again a fair amount back from the target line and turned out toward the target. You should try all these and find what is most comfortable.

Your weight should be on your forward side, almost to the point of having the sensation of leaning toward the target. More than the 70% I recommend for pitch shots. The ball will be about directly in front of the back foot.

Moderately narrow width chipping stance.

Standard width chipping stance.

Very narrow width chipping stance.

The club to use will be the one where the ball is only in the air for about one-third of the total distance to the pin, then rolls to the pin. A six or seven iron might be the choice if the ball is on the opposite side of the green from the pin and the green is long in that direction, or an eight or nine iron, perhaps even pitching wedge, when the green is smaller or the ball is closer to the pin. I use my gap wedge only occasionally, and never use a sand or higher lofted wedge for a chip. Although the distance the ball will roll will be turf-condition dependent (wet or dry, cut short or not, high or low Stimp), the only way to know what club is right for a certain distance is to put in a lot of practice.

As I mentioned in the *Philosophizing* chapter, a chipping stroke can also be used for moderate distances from the green, when the turf is cut short in the area between the ball and the green, and is dry and smooth the entire distance. In that situation a four or five iron may be appropriate, and, though I have not tried it myself, in an era when hybrid clubs are so useful may even mean trying a hybrid for a long chip from well away from the green.

The longer the chip shot, the more I want to move the ball forward in my stance, though not by much, to ensure solid contact at the correct place in the downswing. Not all golfers move the ball forward as I do, however, so try several options and find what works best. Do not think that if you move the ball a bit farther forward your weight distribution will change. The forward weight distribution bias is very important for a reliable, accurate chipping game.

The swing has to be smooth and rhythmic. Repeat. The swing has to be smooth and rhythmic. Nothing moves in the chip swing except the arms and the shoulders. Everything else is motionless. Start the swing with the arms, cock the wrists back slightly—not like we described in the *Arms and Forearms in the Backswing* chapter because this is a much shorter swing—then with barely a brief pause start the downswing to and through the ball. Except for my longest chips, I do not raise the clubhead above the back knee in my backswing. The downswing will be mostly arm and I do not uncock my wrists, but that is a personal thing I have long practiced (As an example of how personal the chip shot is, Jason Day has frequently been noted by TV announcers as having an arms-only chip swing—no wrist action back or forward. It certainly works for him). The swing is a smooth sweeping of the ball through the grass.

A message about the ball in the air one-third of the distance to the hole idea: it depends on the club and the nature of the swing. If the ball flies farther than one-third to the hole, the cause more often than not is a pitch-type swing— not necessarily a problem if the result is what you want. Just be aware it is not the traditional chip swing and outcome.

However you decide to chip, the swing must be repeatable and smooth.

There is one tweak to consider after mastering the basic chipping swing. Swinging the club slightly inside to slightly outside the target line, while maintaining the clubhead on the target line at ball contact, will result in a hook spin. The ball will then roll out to the pin more than it would otherwise. Swinging along the opposite plane, from outside to inside, would in theory make the ball roll less, but I have never heard that better golfers use that technique. The inside-to-outside swing plane is only a slight change from square-to-square, not a significant change from the standard chip swing. Do not try this specialty shot until your chipping game is consistent and does not require conscious thought about everything I have written in this chapter.

Some golfers will choke down on the club, and perhaps bend over slightly for their chip stance; others will always hold the club at the top and stand relatively upright. I recommend the latter—hold the club at the top, stand so your arms can move without being constrained by your body, and change clubs as I've written for the distance of the shot. The result will be a more reliable chipping game.

Chip shots from the side of the green are frequently from an uphill lie. All of the above works, with minor modifications. The sweeping swing is the same, but it is important that the shoulders are parallel to the uphill slope. For an uphill chip I bend my back knee forward to get the parallel to the ground stance. At the same time, and this happens almost automatically with the knee bend, I make sure my weight distribution is appropriately forward. Finally, depending on the amount of slope, the ball made need to be moved more forward in the stance. A couple of practice swings will make clear where the ball should be for the shot you face.

I mentioned Jason Day uses an arms-only chipping style. Other touring pros also chip with an arms-only motion, and it may work for you as well. Take an eight iron for example. The only difference to what I described above is the swing back will have a firm nonbreaking wrist and forearm, and the forward motion through and past contact will also have a nonbreaking wrist and forearm. The tempo of the swing guides the distance the ball goes. A slow-ish tempo will send the ball a relatively short total distance; a faster tempo will provide more force to the ball, which will thus travel farther.

Whichever technique you elect to use, this is not a hard shot. Practice, practice, practice.

Mulligan

Follow the Rules

If you play golf long enough you will be involved in a rules debate with a playing partner or competitor. The issues arising on the PGA Tour during the 2016 season are examples enough it can happen to anyone.

Rules debates come in two colors. A question may arise on where to drop a ball, or on any of the other subjects in the rulebook. Few of us are experts on the entire rulebook and discussions arise. Fair enough. Usually a quick agreement on the course of action results.

The other color of rules issues is more challenging—what to do when someone is not following the rules, especially if it is not your usual group.

A number of years ago I joined a group for a round when I happened to have a day off. I did not know any of the others, but quickly observed one who was the self-designated "best golfer" in the group. It was equally apparent he was in competition with me to maintain his self-designation.

We came to a hard par four. I was on the green putting for par; he was in deep rough off the side of the green. We waited for the other two to play, and then I looked up to watch him play. Magically, his ball was on top of the rough with a smooth easy lie for his chip. I smiled to myself. What to do, what to do?

This was his competition, not mine. I was on a relaxed day off and was not in a mind to make an issue. So I said nothing.

I have not had such an issue arise in a serious competition, happily, and hope never to have one arise—not a conversation anyone would look forward to. My friends and I always play by the rules in our casual and not-so-casual rounds. The rules, after all, are part of the game too.

Take the High Road. Follow the Rules.

The Short Game

Putting

Putting is another part of the game that can be adapted to each golfer's preferences. In fact, not only can it be but it should be adapted to each golfer's preferences. There are recommended "rules" to follow, but the pre-eminent part of the putting game is to be comfortable over the ball.

The putting game also provides another example of how much golf has changed over the years. The 50s and 60s putting style is unheard of today—hunched over stance, arms nearly locked to the body, the swing nearly all wrists. Today we see the opposite.

First the grip. The knuckles visible approach does not apply. Most putters have a square or rectangular club grip and the best way to hold the putter is to have both thumbs point straight down the grip, thus making the palms of the two hands face each other in a parallel position. The meat of the lower thumb will be directly on top of the upper thumb.

A second difference from the description in *The Grip* chapter is that instead of the little finger on the lower hand overlapping on top of the other hand, the reverse should occur. The first finger of the upper hand should comfortably rest over the top of and between the last two fingers of the lower hand. Some golfers have that finger overlap the lower hand and point down the shaft.

Do not have your lower hand's forefinger point straight down the putter. I did this for a long time, but eventually realized the forefinger can tend to over-control the clubhead, something to avoid. We want both hands to work together as a unit.

The stance should be shoulder width, square to the line of the putt, though the forward foot can be pulled back from the target line. I prefer to try to be perfectly square to the target line.

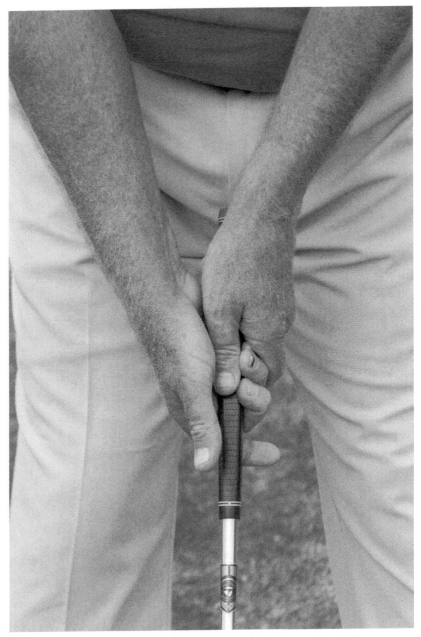

Putting grip – palms facing each other, thumbs point down shaft.

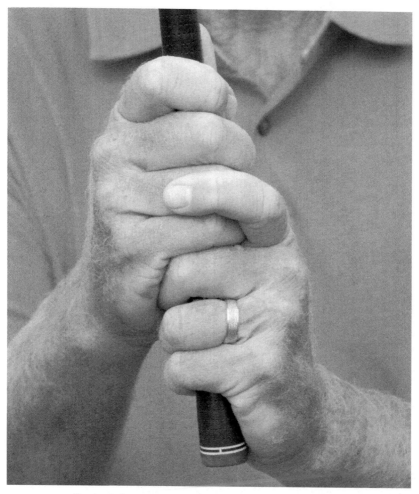

Putting grip – little finger of upper hand over lower hand.

The recommended ball position—forward-to-back—for putting has changed over the years. When I was young we were told to have the ball directly below our eyes, more specifically the forward eye. Today the focus is more on being comfortable over the ball. I usually have the ball in line with my forward eye, but farther out away from my body and therefore not directly below the eye. For me, this puts the ball about one-third of the way back from my forward foot. Some golfers have the ball farther forward, others farther back. Ball position on the green is a personal decision, of course, though I don't think the ball should be too far away from being in line with the forward eye.

The distance of the ball from the front of the body is also a comfort issue. If you find the putter frequently moves out away from your body at the start of the swing, try moving the ball farther from your feet.

The stance should be upright, the arms hanging comfortably down, not constrained close to the body, and the body's weight balanced from forward to backward and from front to rear. A bottom line description of the putting stance is balanced comfort.

The putting swing is a pendulum movement, with no body motion other than from the shoulders down through the arms and hands. There is no wrist cocking or uncocking. The pendulum stroke is smoothly back and forward through contact with the ball. The follow-through should be longer than the backswing.

A reason the preferred stance today is upright and not hunched over is so the pendulum-like swing will not be constrained by the body. A hunched-over body does not allow the arms and shoulders to move as easily and as smoothly as is necessary for a consistent putting game.

The clubhead should sit on the ground when addressing the ball, with the toe of the clubhead not much, if at all, off the ground. There are a few pros who have the heel of the clubhead on the ground, but not the rest of the clubhead. It is hard to putt consistently with that clubhead position. If your putter is not comfortable when square to the ground, consider having your pro adjust the lie of the club, or find a new putter that is better suited to your swing's characteristics.

You may have read the backswing should be one-third the length of the swing after contact with the ball. I focus on a smooth backswing and a smooth

Pendulum putting backstroke.

Putting stance.

Pendulum putting forward stroke.

follow-through with the back and forward lengths adapted to the length of the putt. My putting swing key is to make sure I do not quit on the ball before a smooth clean contact occurs.

I see quite a few golfers who have a rather long backswing for all putts, and have to adapt for short or mid-length putts by slowing the clubhead down before contact with the ball on the downswing. There is no way to be consistent with that technique. Go practice short putts with a short backswing and a smooth, firm follow-through, then practice increasingly longer putts with a slightly longer backswing and follow-through. Before long you will realize this approach leads to better putting consistency.

Note, though, that for even longer putts it is best not to further lengthen the backswing and downswing. Instead, distance control is best on longer putts through use of more force imparted to the clubhead by the hands and arms, while maintaining a controlled length of both the backswing and the follow-through.

More than anything else, we want the putting swing to be smooth, unconstrained, and require the optimum amount of energy to be imparted to the ball for the distance that is the length of the putt. Everything I have just described, from grip to stance to ball position to the shoulder-based pendulum swing, combine for a consistent putting game.

Mulligan

Two Putting Tips

No Crabbing on the Green Either

The *Mulligan* titled *No Crabbing* said, essentially, "Get your feet in position and leave them there. Period." A similar, but not exactly the same, message is important to the on-the-green part of the game.

You just read my words "The stance should be ... square to the line of the putt ...." And it should be. But what do most golfers do?

The on-the-green sequence for most amateur golfers is to stand behind the ball, read the break, walk to the ball and set the stance and grip in place while looking at the hole, adjust the clubface while looking at the line the ball is intended to roll on, and make the putt.

What is wrong with that sequence? What is wrong is the setting of the stance and the looking at the line the ball is intended to roll on must be simultaneous. The proper putting stance is aligned with the line of the putt, not the line to the hole. How many times have you heard a golfer say "I did not read enough break?" My observation more often than not is the alignment was wrong. The stance was crabbed compared to the desired line of the putt.

Reading putts may be a problem on the big breaking sidewinders we see on television, more often, hopefully, than we experience. But crabbing the stance on those putts is not as often a problem. When we have those putts, we know inherently the putt line is nowhere near the line to the hole, and most of the time we get the alignment at least more-or-less correct. Putts with more subtle breaks are harder to read, harder to set up for, and harder to putt generally. So, for putts with a relatively small break, make sure your stance is square to the line the ball is to start rolling on. Then the only worry is the speed. So much easier.

Smooth, Soft, Silky

In the *Mulligan* titled *Don't Strangle the Grip*, I wrote "Tension does not work in golf. Mental tension does not work. Physical tension does not work. Relaxation is a key to success in this game. It must start with relaxation in the hands and forearms." Those words are nowhere more important than on the putting green.

In recent years I have been very erratic on the greens. A round with less than 36 putts has at times been a goal seemingly never again to be attained. I have come to realize that my putting challenges have been made worse by the mental and physical tension that poor putting causes when I pull the putter out of my golf bag. Not a good thing.

Focus on holding the putter very softly. Do not hold the club tight in any way—you want to feel almost as if the club is barely in your hands. Your pendulum putting stroke should be silky-smooth, back and forward with soft hands, no tension, and almost robotic in its look and feel.

I find that when I practice a soft, silky-smooth, putting stroke, I frequently do not hit the ball far enough. Distance control is harder when I focus on this putting stroke style. That challenge can be overcome with practice, and you will find that it is not hard to master distance control with this putting stroke.

The good news is that the soft, silky-smooth, putting stroke makes short putts much easier to make. That is my recent finding and with practice it will be yours as well.

The Short Game

Sand Play

When I wrote "This is without a doubt the hardest chapter for me to write" at the beginning of *The Wrists and Forearms in the Backswing* chapter, I lied. This is harder. The difference is, when it comes to the wrists and forearms, I feel like I have always figured out what to do and how to do it, even if it was hard or if I did not do it as well as I would like. Sand play has always been more of a struggle. The course I grew up on had few traps. The other courses I played had more traps, but few were in play. So I grew up not practicing sand shots. I have continued that mistake throughout my life.

In truth, these shots are not hard. I have learned that truth from those time periods when I do practice from the sand. The pros are good, or great, in the sand because they practice these not hard shots. They should not be so much of a challenge for us either, even if we may not get as good as the men and women on television. So my first message is to practice your sand game.

What we need to understand is how sand shots are different from other shots. The first difference is, after all the discussion of how to hit the ball solidly and crisply, we don't do either from the sand—in fact we do not hit the ball at all. As you likely know, successful sand shots are carried out by having the club contact the sand several inches behind the ball.

A second difference is we should not have our eyes locked on the back of the ball. Instead, our eyes should be locked on the point behind the ball where we want the club to contact the sand. In a sense this is no different from other shots we take—in all cases our eyes should be locked on the spot we want the club to contact, ball or sand.

Third, although we want the lower body working to our benefit for other swings, we want to carry out sand shots with a quiet lower body. That change is not hard, but it does mean the swing needs to be adjusted if we are to be reliably successful from the sand.

Fourth, and this is tied into the quiet lower body issue, sand shots require we fully continue our swings through the sand, past the point where the ball was sitting, into a full follow-through. The sand shots I am talking about are those from bunkers near the green; our pitch and chip shots from the grass for the same distance do not always require a full follow-through. From the sand it is the opposite—a full follow-through is absolutely essential.

Those are a few of the obvious differences between a 25 yard pitch shot from the fairway or rough and a 25 yard sand shot. To understand the other differences, and to understand why we do what we have to do to be successful, let's move on to the theory of the sand shot.

I wrote a few pages ago to forget the divot, but when we use our wedges for pitch shots of almost any distance, our swing generally does result in a divot after contact with the ball. The divot is the result of the setup of the stance, the setting of the bottom edge of the club on the ground at address, and the path of, and the wrist and forearm action in, the swing, all of which lead to direct contact with the ball by a club on a downward path. The downward path causes the bottom edge of the club to dig into the ground after contact with the ball. In principle, we could probably use the same technique for sand shots under twenty yards in length or so, but a forceful swing would be required to dig through the sand, making distance control difficult. By relying on the design of the sand club we have an easier way to get up and down from the sand.

The easier way is not to make contact with the ball at all, only the sand. How? The short answer is to adjust our stance and swing so the club is not on a downward path, but rather involves more of a glancing blow slicing through the sand. If we properly adjust our grip and stance, we can learn to carry out these shots just like we see on television.

Start with the grip. We cannot grip the club so the face is in its normal angle relative to the ground, with the bottom edge, the bounce, directly touching the ground as it does for a standard pitch shot. What we need to do is decrease the angle relative to the ground, and changing the grip is the first step in decreasing that angle. The clubhead should be opened to be face up, as if to lay on the ground, then, with the club in that position, gripped as normal. The result is a

Sand play - correct clubhead position.

Sand play - incorrect clubhead position.

grip that makes it much harder for the hands to turn the club over, which would cause digging down into the sand, not slicing through it.

Next the stance is adjusted—to further increase the slicing action. First, address the ball as normal, with the feet aligned along the target line, the ball in the center of the stance, and the club gripped with the face open, as described above. Then pull the forward foot toward the rear so a line from the back foot to the forward foot makes about a 30° angle with the target line. The exact angle can be adjusted for comfort and the distance of the shot to be carried out. The resulting ball position is relatively far forward in the stance.

Finally, the swing must have the clubhead going back along the backward extension of the target line, and returning toward the ball along the same path. Doing so, in combination with the grip and the stance adjustments, allows the bottom edge of the clubhead, the bounce, to approach the sand at a very low angle. That low angle allows the club to slice into the sand behind the ball, and continue through the sand past the point at which the ball sits. The force of the sand's movement as the club moves forward down the target line is what causes the ball to move forward towards the target.

All this leaves the question of how far behind the ball the club should contact the sand. Among the guidance of the golf books or articles you may have read is (i) the contact point should be "one credit card's length behind the ball," or (ii) "you should pretend the ball is sitting on George Washington's head on a dollar bill and the contact point should be the back edge of the dollar bill," or (iii) "the contact point should be two ball's width behind the ball." My answer is about one to four inches behind the ball, depending on how fluffy the sand is and how far the shot is.

It is important to maintain body stability and keep the lower body quiet during sand shots. Using a wider stance than for any other shot of the same length, thus keeping the center of gravity low, ensures body stability. The sand shot stance is certainly one in which the feeling of almost but not quite starting to sit down is in the legs and hips. Maintaining that feeling throughout the swing will go a long way to a successful sand shot.

Preparing for sand stance.
Clubface open, stance square.

Final sand stance.
Open clubface, front foot pulled back from target line.

The body's weight needs to be biased forward more for sand shots than it is for shots of the same length from grass.

All this adds up to a weakened grip, an open clubface, a wider and lower stance pointed about 30° to the inside of the target line, and a quiet, weight biased forward, lower body. Is there anything else to be done besides looking at the sand one to four inches behind the ball to improve the odds of successfully completing the shot? Yes, of course there is.

For most sand shots, the way to maintain the quiet lower body and to ensure the club contacts the sand in the place and at the angle we want is to have an early wrist cock and a swing path more upright and narrower than for other shots. These points increase the likelihood the club will slice into the sand along the path we want it to follow.

Early cocking of the wrists mean the swing arc will not be as wide as for other shots of the same length. As the sand shot length increases, the wrist cock will have to be later, and the swing arc wider, to ensure the necessary power is imparted to the sand. In any case, however, a full follow-through is essential. The follow-through is the time in a sand shot where the lower body does finally come into play, as the legs flow forward with the arms and the club into the final pose we all hope to have after a successful sand shot.

Sand play is different from other shots of the same distance for all these reasons. Thus our need to practice them more, not less.

Mulligan

It is Not Always
Going to Work

I played a vacation round recently at one of the fine courses associated with the American Club in Kohler, Wisconsin. Whistling Straits, where the PGA Championship was held a few years ago, is one of those courses. It was a good day—perfect temperature, clear skies, no wind. I hit the ball well—hit fifteen fairways and greens. I missed one par three green by three or four yards, had one ball on a par four land in the fairway but bounce barely into the rough, and similarly only missed one par five green in regulation, and that by just a few yards. Should have been a great day.

I did not make one putt of any length, and missed many in the range of three to six feet. The greens were challenging, but this was not a problem with the greens. I just could not get the ball into the hole.

We are all going to have days like this, hopefully infrequently. But what to do when today is the day?

On vacation with friends, what we should all do, and what I hope I did, was enjoy the day, enjoy the camaraderie, enjoy the shots that did go well. I tried my best to see what was going on with the putter, but mostly I tried to enjoy the day.

Years ago I would not have had the patience to hold myself together on a day like I had in Wisconsin, and we have all seen golfers who do not hold it together. Best just to enjoy the day. We are amateurs—it is not always going to work like we want it to.

Your Practice Regimen

The challenges of life force us all into periods when we do not get to play very often. Those periods usually do not let us get to the driving range either. What to do when you do get back to the course or the range?

As I write this I am ending a nearly two year period in which I have only fifteen rounds on my handicap card. I have played a few rounds in recent weeks, and find I have a lot of work to do to get my game back. Range time is needed.

Don't start pounding balls endlessly on the range without a goal in mind. Have an objective to work on. I usually focus on two long-in-place weaknesses in my game. By now you know what they are. I have an arm-focused swing, with weak and inconsistent wrist action. I also have always had an issue with keeping my back leg in position in my backswing. Combined, these problems lead to an upright swing plane with inconsistent ball contact and inconsistent distances. What better time to work on these problems than when returning to the game after a long layoff?

I start with my wedges, the short pitch shots we all need to be able to play. The distances I am talking about are from about twenty yards to about fifty yards. I have written in earlier pages about my poor wrist and forearm action, and starting to work on short wedge shots is a good way to remind my body of what it should be doing when I swing the club. The other advantage of starting with short wedge shots is they are a good way to get the body tuned up with the tempo and rhythm of your game.

My practice regimen is straightforward. The gap wedge is first, because the range I practice on has a practice green at the distance I usually hit that club. I follow my on-the-course routine—setting my stance, weight distribution and body position, focusing on my rhythm and tempo, then continue in tempo down and through the ball. In the back of my mind is also my wrist action issue. Thoughts of this kind are in my mind all the way through my bag, up to the driver, during each practice session.

All of this is for the practice range; golfers should know what swing thoughts need to be worked on during a routine practice session, or in warm up for a round.

No golfer can—and certainly should not—think about all these things on the golf course itself. The purpose of the range is to make the swing second nature so the only real thought on the course is to repeat what was practiced without thinking about all the details. You will be at the point where your range work has been a success when the swing occurs naturally, without all of those thoughts in mind. Then the only thing left is to take it to the course. Which is where you want to be anyway, right?

Mulligan

When to Leave the Driving Range

I have always liked going to the practice range. I often go to the course without even thinking about playing a round because I like the repetition of hitting balls and working on what I need to work on. But I learned long ago not to make the mistake of staying on the range at the wrong time—there are times to leave the range early without completing the focused work that was planned for the day.

Golf is an intellectually-oriented game requiring a completely golf-centered mind. I am writing this after having left the range because I could not maintain a golf-centered mind. Remember the *Mulligan* titled *Concentrate*? It applies to the range as well.

You should also leave the range to avoid practicing swing problems. Time spent on the practice range should be used to focus on improving an aspect of the game that is known to need improvement. But when you do not really know what the problem is, or how to correct it, you should go home. The biggest mistake one can make is staying on the range pounding balls without knowing whether the problem is being solved. The most likely result those days is to end up reinforcing bad habits, and once reinforced bad habits are that much harder to correct.

So, if you are having a bad day on the range, go home.

My Swing Sequence

Full Swing Sequence 1 – Quiet body as arms start back.

Full Swing Sequence 3 – Head, back leg, and side remain in position.

Full Swing Sequence 2 – Club points nearly straight back,
forward knee has begun to point behind ball.

Full Swing Sequence 4 – Shoulder turn nearly complete, head,
back leg, and side in position, wrists nearly fully cocked.

Full Swing Sequence 5 – Club at top of backswing is just short of horizontal; head has not moved, left knee points well behind ball.

Full Swing Sequence 7 – Hip movement continues, little change in arms-to-club relative position.

Full Swing Sequence 6 – Swing starts down with hip movement,
arms-to-club relative position unchanged.

Full Swing Sequence 8 – Hips out of way, enabling full arm extension.

Full Swing Sequence 9 – Weight on outside of forward foot, back foot nearly off ground, head position nearly unchanged.

Full Swing Sequence 10 – Head follows arm movement upward toward finish.

Full Swing Sequence 11 – High arm finish, club wrapped around shoulders,
Body vertical and facing toward target.

Source Material and Acknowledgments

As I wrote in the Preface, I have accumulated a thick notebook of golf clippings over the years. I also have a box of golf magazines in my study, and a library of books from various eras on my bookshelf. The question arises as to which of these I have relied on in getting my thoughts on these pages.

The answer is all, none, or I don't know. If one does anything for long, and then tries to put to print what he thinks he knows, he is almost by definition at a loss to know what his source material is. Or, better said, his source material is the accumulated knowledge he has gained over the years and can pull into the forefront of his consciousness to put the words to paper. If you agree with that statement, I do not need to try to put any references down as my source material. Perhaps this is also why none of the golf books on my bookshelf have a bibliography. The fact I am an amateur and the authors of those books are professionals does not change the mental state I was in, as compared to them, when I wrote this book.

But what I have written does not mean the substance of this book is not similar to what might be found in my clippings, golf magazines, or books. For example, as I prepared to write this chapter, I pulled out my copy of Tom Watson's *Getting Back to Basics* and was shocked to find the table of contents is similar in structure to the table of contents of this book. I wrote my table of contents years ago and had no idea of the similarity. Did I unwittingly copy that book's structure, or did my reading of the book long ago, along with the other things I have read over the years, put in my mind the same structure for analysis of the game Hall of Fame member Tom Watson used? I do not know the answer. I have not read that book in years, not because it is not an excellent book but because I have more recently been thinking about my own views on how to play the game.

Similarly with my file of golf clippings. The reason I pulled out my copy of *Getting Back to Basics* was I happened to see a newspaper clipping in it acting as a bookmark. It was from Jack Nicklaus's newspaper column, published more than twenty-five years ago—I know the age as the paper it was published in went out of business at least that long ago. The clipping's words are eerily similar to what I have written in several of the pages in this book. Mr. Nicklaus certainly wrote a clear and concise column, as his messages were in my writing mind even if the clipping was not.

None of this is intended to say I have not gone to my notebook for research on the topics I have written about. For certain chapters I had to do a lot of thinking on what to say, for example for the *Sand Play* chapter. But even then it is not clear to me what I should, or should not, explicitly reference in these pages. My research on sand play led me to find a clipping of an article by Byron Nelson giving guidance in part at odds with a clipping of an article by Nick Faldo. The fact what I have written is closer to Byron Nelson's guidance does not mean I did not learn something from Nick Faldo. Do I reference one, the other, or both? I am not sure.[3] In the end, my bibliography includes articles I recall looking at more than once over the years, even though in most cases I did not refer to them until after the writing process was over and I was putting together the bibliography.

What all this means, I think, is—as I wrote in the *Preface*—this book is a combination of all the readings I have done over the years, what I have learned from my own practice and study of the game, what I have learned directly or indirectly from professionals I have known and taken lessons from, and what I have learned by observation of those with whom I have played golf. I have all those sources, and in particular the professionals who have taught me personally, for my knowledge. I hope these pages have conveyed that knowledge in a way that will be an aid to those of you who enjoy the game as much as I do.

Every author has people to thank for helping him get his idea for a book into a form that can be published. My first thought for this book was so my sister Jean, her husband Jeff, and their two boys, David and Rob, would have

---

[3] Truth be told, after much thought about the Nelson and Faldo articles, I think the intent was for them both to say the same thing, but the structure/editing of the language left a question in my mind. Not a bad thing, to spend extra time on a topic that needs further thought for many reasons.

something from me about this game that has taken so much of my leisure time for so many years. The first edition, released only to them under the title *Uncle Steve's Guide to Golf*, took much longer than I had planned but was truly a labor of love. That labor led to *The Thinking Golfer's Manual*, which is different from the *Guide* in many ways. It too has been a labor of love.

This book would not have the look it does without the superb photography of David W. Clements, and the photo editing of his colleague E. J. Taul. I cannot thank them enough for their help making my swing demonstrate the points I have tried to make in this book.

I want to thank in particular the helpful editing and comments from Karen Koerner, Rodger Koerner, and Wyatt Koerner, whose positive vibes enabled me to take this book to its final form. I owe Karen particular thanks for forcing me to think about what title to publish this book under; the words on the cover come from her suggestions.

This book's final form would never have occurred but for the push on the home front from my wife Aimee Katherine.

Stephen Koch
October, 2017

Bibliography

Cook, Chuck, "Are You a Swinger or a Hitter," *Golf Digest*, 1992, 68-76.

Cook, Chuck, "One Move for Power," *Golf Digest*, October, 1993, 60-69.

Crafter, Jane, "How to Hole Them from 6 Feet and In," *Golf Digest*, March 1997, 145-152.

Davenport, Scott, "The Key to Distance: Swing Down in Sequence," *Golf Digest*, January 1993, 66-69.

Els, Ernie, "How to Make Your Tempo Silky Smooth," Golf Digest, May, 1996, 52-59.

Els, Ernie, " 'Straight' Talk about my Left Arm," *Golf Digest*, June 1996, 70-71.

Faldo Nick and David Leadbetter, "Lengthen your flat spot—and your drives," *Golf Digest*, February, 1995, 40.

Faldo, Nick, "My Complete Guide to Bunker Play," *Golf Digest*, July, 1992, 62-66.

Faldo, Nick, "Pitching It Close," *Golf Digest*, September, 1993, 46-53.

Faldo, Nick, *The Faldo Fundamentals*, Faldo Golf Institute by Marriott, undated.

Flick, Jack, "Release, Which One is Right for You?" *Golf Digest*, August, 1992, 72-79.

Gladwell, Malcolm, *The Tipping Point, How Little Things Can Make a Big Difference*, Little Brown, 2000.

Golf Magazine, *Your Long Game*, Award Books, 1968.

Golf Digest, *How to Solve Your Golf Problems*, Cornerstone Library Publications, 1969.

Haney, Hank, "Back to Putting Basics," *Golf Digest*, December, 1994, 72-75.

Haney, Hank, "Bunker Basics," *Golf Digest*, September, 1996, 86-88.

Harmon, Butch, "Get Out of Sand with One Hand," *Golf Digest*, November, 1997, 64-71.

Hogan, Ben, *Five Lessons—The Modern Fundamentals of Golf*, Simon and Schuster, 1985 (first published by Simon & Schuster, 1957).

Hogan, Ben, *Power Golf*, Pocket Books, 1957, (first published by A.S. Barnes and Company, Inc. 1948).

Johnson, Hank, "How to Take Dead Aim," *Golf Digest*, April 1994, 66-71.

Kostis, Peter, "Beth Daniel: A Model to Draw From," *Golf Digest*, May, 1996, 82-83.

Kostis, Peter, "How to Hold the Club," *Golf Digest*, April, 1994, 54.

Kostis, Peter, "The Power of Balance," *Golf Digest*, March 1995, 134-145.

Leadbetter, David, "Pitch it with Your Body," *Golf Digest*, March, 1993, 73-79.

Mahoney, Tim, "Chip Away at Your Full-Swing Faults," *Golf Digest*, October, 1991, 86-88.

Mahoney, Tim, "S P A C E Out Your Swing," *Golf Digest*, February, 1998, 60-63.

Mallon, Meg, "Make 'Em All," *Golf Digest*, November, 1995, 96-100.

Mickelson, Phil, "You Can Hole Every Putt," *Golf Digest*, April, 1997, 75-82.

Nelson Byron, "Stay 'down and through' with long irons," *Golf Digest,* May 1995, 52.

Nicklaus, Jack, "Arm 'pictures' promote use of both sides," *Golf Digest*, November, 1992.

Nicklaus, Jack, "Shove your butt out for better turn," *Golf Digest*, March, 1992, 41.

Nicklaus, Jack, "Start back 'ridiculously' slowly," *Golf Digest*, September, 1992, 29.

Nicklaus, Jack, "Tilt the triangle for correct shoulder slant," *Golf Digest*, December 1991, 25.

Nicklaus, Jack, "Three keys on the follow-through," *Golf Digest*, August, 1992, 26.

Owens, Dr. Dede, "How to Hit the Longer Irons", *Golf Digest*, March 1992, 132-133.

Palmer, Arnold, *The Arnold Palmer Method*, Dell Publishing, 1968.

Palmer, Arnold, *My Game and Yours*, Fireside Books, 1983.

Price, Nick, "Dead Solid Putting," *Golf Digest*, September, 1993, 67-73.

Trevino, Lee, "Hit down with fairway woods," *Golf Digest*, January, 1995, 54.

Trulock, Judy, "Hit sand shots 'right on the money'," *Golf Digest*, August, 1996, 48.

Watson, Tom, "A good swing has two starts," *Golf Digest*, July 1995, 30.

Watson, Tom, "Davis Love's Power Secret," *Golf Digest*, January 1998, 26.

Watson, Tom, "For crisper chips, copy Langer's strong grip," *Golf Digest*, February, 1998, 30.

Watson, Tom, "Grip down the same on all chipping clubs," *Golf Digest*, November, 1997, 34.

Watson, Tom, "Rule No. 1 in Chipping," *Golf Digest.Com,* April, 2014, 60.

Watson, Tom, "Study Couples' modern finish," *Golf Digest*, August, 1992, 32.

Watson, Tom, "Watch the sand, not the ball," *Golf Digest*, July, 1997, 30.

Watson, Tom, "Weight better toward toes than heels," *Golf Digest*, September, 1992, 44.

Watson, Tom, "Why the 'Short thumb' is better," *Golf Digest*, March, 1992, 44.

Watson, Tom, *Getting Back to Basics*, NYT Special Services, Inc. and Pocket Books, 1992.

Watson, Tom, *Getting Up and Down*, Vintage Books, 1983.

Watson, Tom, *Tom Watson's Strategic Golf*, NYT Special Services, Inc. and Pocket Books, 1993.

Woods, Tiger, "Grip club 'strong' for distance and control," *Golf Digest*, 1997, 26-27.

Woods, Tiger, "How and when to chip with your 3-wood," *Golf Digest*, September, 1997, 24-25.

Index

ABOUT THE AUTHOR

Steve Koch plays out of the Grand Pines Golf Club in Montgomery, Texas. He retired on Independence Day, July 4, 2015, after a career in science, engineering, and the law.

Over the course of his career, he maintained an interest in, if not always having the time to dedicate himself to, the game of golf, which he started playing in his home town of Fort Wayne, Indiana at the age of nine. *The Thinking Golfer's Manual* is the result of his study of the game during all the years in which the thought to actually spend time on a golf course was largely a dream.

He received engineering and science degrees from Purdue University, the Massachusetts Institute of Technology, and the Woods Hole Oceanographic Institute, and a law degree from the University of Houston Law Center. He has publications in statistics, oceanography, ocean engineering, and the law. All of his career-developed skills were essential to the writing of this book.

He lives outside of Houston, Texas with his wife and the manager of the household, a cat named Maximilian Bonaparte.